D0874219

"Topside green diver, the tunnel collapsed. I repeat the tunnel collapsed." There I was seventy feet down with twenty feet of mud on top of me.

I didn't panic, in fact, it didn't initially register that I was in danger. But the moment the master diver spoke to me, I could tell he was concerned. "You okay, Ricky?"

"Yes, Master Diver, I'm okay, but I can't move."

It was as if I was in cement and my legs and arms–even my fingers—were frozen in place.

"Ricky, turn the witch back on."

"I can't move."

In truth, I was never worried about my predicament. I wasn't hurt, I had plenty of air. I was just locked in mud 70' down.

I remained surprisingly calm and relaxed inside the collapsed tunnel. To some extent, I felt safe in my muddy hole like a mud-crab. I started moving one finger on my left hand, which was near my stomach, then I could move two fingers, and soon I was moving all four fingers, as if I was waving.

Now I was on a mission. I was pushing forward toward the valve, but I was also getting cold, very cold. It was a race against time, which I would experience many times to come in my life.

Finally, I reached the valve and exclaimed I was ready to turn the witch back on, I was shivering uncontrollably, which made talking difficult. But I exclaimed, I was not leaving that hole until a diver handed me the recovery line.

The master diver said, "Ricky, don't worry about that. We need to get you out of the water. You have already omitted several hours of decompression and you must be freezing."

"Then a couple more minutes won't matter," I responded with my teeth chattering.

BREATHE

A MASTER DIVER'S SURVIVAL TALES

RICK BETTUA

WITH

ROB MACGREGOR

I would like to dedicate this book to my three sons
Nicholas, Troy and Derek
"I wrote this book for you, love dad"

I would like to thank the following people
who helped me with his endeavor

Angela Bettua
Glenn Dickson
Helen Curnock
Kim Cousins
Thomas Stevens
All the Sailors and Marines that made this possible

PREFACE

Rick Bettua should be dead. Many times over.

The retired U.S. Navy diver suffered a devastating attack by a twelve-foot bull shark that shredded his thigh from his knee to his hip. By the time he reached the shore ninety minutes later, he'd bled out, he had no pulse and wasn't breathing. Yet, emergency medical workers didn't give up. His miraculous recovery in late 2020 was just the most recent of his numerous underwater life-and-death experiences.

BREATHE is Rick Bettua's survival story. It's also a story about perseverance against great odds, and his impressive skills to solve problems—and even save lives—under extreme conditions. It begins and ends with the shark attack and his recovery that defied the odds.

In between are fifteen other stories in which Bettua narrowly escaped death during his remarkable thirty-two-year Navy career. In one instance, in a search for a lost piece of a propeller, he was buried alive seventy feet below the surface and under twenty feet of mud when a tunnel collapsed. When he finally worked his way free after two hours, he then completed the task, so no other divers would be endangered.

The first-person narration takes the reader through Rick Bettua's evolution as a diver from a kid spearfishing to one of the elite Navy master divers. He never wasted time to achieve a goal. As a twelve-year-old, he joined a spear fishing club on his own, then the Navy when he was just seventeen.

Aided by his love of diving and his determination to be the best at whatever he pursued, he moved rapidly ahead in his career. He became a master diver only one year after becoming a chief petty officer. He achieved the highest rank possible for an enlisted sailor, master chief, at age thirty-three, one of the youngest ever to attain that rank.

But Bettua's promotions never kept him out of the water– or out of perilous circumstances. His skills, his fearlessness and his perseverance helped him survive time and time again throughout his career, and beyond it. But I'll let Rick tell his story.

Rob MacGregor

ENLISTED RANKS NAVY / MARINE CORPS

E-1 Seaman Recruit / Private
E-2 Seaman Apprentice / Private First Class
E-3 SeamanLance / Corporal
E-4 Petty Officer Third Class / Corporal
E-5 Petty Officer Second Class / Sergeant
E-6 Petty Officer First Class / Staff Sergeant
E-7 Chief Petty Officer / Gunnery Sergeant
E-8 Senior Chief Petty Officer / Master Sergeant
E-9 Master Chief Petty Officer / Sergeant Major

OFFICER RANKS NAVY / MARINE CORPS

O-1 EnsignSecond / Lieutenant
O-2 Lieutenant Junior Grade / First Lieutenant
O-3 Lieutenant / Captain
O-4 Lieutenant Commander / Major
O-5 Commander / Lieutenant Colonel
O-6 Captain / Colonel
O-7 Rear Admiral / (Lower)Brigadier General
O-8 Rear Admiral / Major General
O-9 Vice Admiral / Lieutenant General
O-10 AdmiralGeneral
Chief of Naval Operations / Commandant

CHAPTER 1

THE DAY I DIED

25 Oct 2020

If we'd only skipped the last dive, I thought, pulling myself into the boat.

"You have three minutes…three minutes to save my life," I told my dive partner as he quickly climbed aboard. I was bleeding profusely from two shark bites that had shredded my thigh from the hip to the knee. I tried to stay calm and told him to make a tourniquet from his weight belt.

The day had begun with a beautiful sunrise. The seventeen-foot boat bounded across the ocean heading east toward Britomart Reef that was twenty miles off-shore. It looked as if it was going to be a perfect day. Upon arriving at the southern end of the reef, we anchored at a familiar bommie (reef) that normally produces some quality fish. But after stepping overboard, we noticed the water was dirty and there were very few fish.

Then we headed north, hitting spot after spot and with each dive, Pete and I noticed the visibility was getting better and better the further north we went. We finally got to the northern end of Britomart Reef and the water was crystal clear. We anchored and slid into the water and the first thing we saw were two very large bull sharks on the bottom moving slowly. This is a common occurrence here, so we didn't think anything about it.

We saw no fish so started swimming back to the boat. When I turned to look behind me there was a dark shape over five feet wide and twenty-five feet long. At first it startled me due to its size, and that it was coming toward me. Then I noticed it was a very friendly whale shark. I passed my speargun from my right hand to my left and extended my right hand as if to say stop. Much to my surprise, she came all the way up to my hand like an old friend and I touched her. I gave her a gentle rub and she slowly turned and swam away. Whale sharks are very rare here, so it was either a spectacular sight, a warning, or maybe both.

Pete and I got into the boat, laughing and hoping one of us got the whale shark on Go Pro. I said we better head back to shore. The wind was picking up, but Pete wanted to dive one more spot.

"Hey, we've got enough fish. Let's just go."

He laughed and said it was only about a hundred yards away. We anchored directly over the bommie, which was only about thirty-six feet deep. It was situated in the middle of a huge white sandy area that dropped off to about seventy feet.

As we got into the water, the spot was alive with quality fish. I picked one out, and made a slow dive down, taking my time not to spook the fish. I aimed my spear and clicked. The fish felt nothing and was dead on impact. I swam over to grab the shaft, and that's when I spotted a twelve-foot bull shark coming over the top of the bommie, straight for me.

The shark was massive, probably six hundred pounds. Its head was huge, and it was rushing toward me at a tremendous speed. I smashed it in the face with my speargun as hard as I could, but it had no effect. Instinctively, I rolled right and that's when the behemoth sunk its jaws into my left thigh, not once, but twice. Then it turned 180 degrees, giving me a full view of its massive size, then left just as fast as it came.

Everything was in slow motion and in my mind I said, "That thing just bit me." I repeated it as a cloud of blood enveloped me. I was thirty-six feet down, and I knew I was in trouble. My thirty-two years of naval training kicked in, and I calmly said to myself, *Rick get out of the water.*

As I swam up, Pete grabbed me near the surface. So much blood was pouring out of my leg that I couldn't even see my fins. It was a horrific attack, and my left leg was shredded. All I could see was blood and I was worried the shark would return to finish what it started. Using just my arms, I climbed up into the boat, where I fell into a lounger. Once Pete was in the boat I calmly said, "Three minutes, Pete. You've got three minutes."

"What for, Rick?"

"You have three minutes to save my life. Take your weight belt off, strip the weights off, then put it as high as you can on my thigh, and get it tight."

He worked as fast as he could, but the makeshift tourniquet wasn't tight enough, and the blood was still flowing. I told him to take my weight belt and do the same but get it tighter. He pulled so hard on the second belt, that it snapped.

During my years in the Navy, I received countless hours of medical training, specifically related to traumas, such as casualties related to IEDs—Improved Explosive Devices. We practiced over and over how to make a tourniquet, and how to apply one. We were taught when applying them, tighten them up until the patient screams, then go two more turns.

During the practice, the trainers would shout, "Hurry up. Three minutes, you only have three minutes before your patient will bleed out from a damaged femoral artery." They also made us aware that by using a tourniquet you were more than likely to cause the removal of that limb, depending upon the evacuation time.

Ironically, three years earlier, I saved a man's life who had been attacked by a bull shark on a reef in the same area. His thigh and calf were mutilated, and I'd applied two tourniquets to keep him alive until we reached shore. But he still lost his leg.

I knew the remaining makeshift tourniquet was not tight enough, and I asked Pete for my bag. Inside it, I had a satellite phone. I wanted to call Angela and the kids so I could say I loved them. However, so much blood was pouring out of me, I couldn't focus to push the buttons. One second the buttons would be clear, and the next the entire phone would look blurry. I couldn't even push the two preset buttons. I threw it down in frustration, and said, "Tell Angela and the kids I love them and that I am sorry.

"Why *sorry*, Rick?" Pete asked as he pulled up the anchor.

"Because I might not be there for them growing up."

I love all three of my sons equally, and my wife dearly, but I kept thinking of my youngest son, Derek. We have a special bond, and I knew he would take it the hardest. Derek was only six, and he still slept with his daddy. With tears just streaming down my face, I knew I had to survive for all of them. But it would take more than what I had. I knew I needed a miracle.

Pete started the engine and we headed back to shore. Within minutes, we saw a much larger craft that was out fishing. Pete pulled up to the boat and screamed there had been a shark attack. One of the men dove in the water and came aboard. He told me his name was Ben and he was a pediatric cardiologist. Ben called to his two friends that I was in a bad way, then they all transferred me into the larger boat.

They laid me on the deck of the boat on my back, and immediately it was as if an elephant was standing on my chest. "I can't breathe! I can't breathe!" I called out, so they cut my wetsuit jacket off me, but it didn't help. I was having a heart attack, even though I knew I had a strong heart.

I attempted to escape the pain by rolling over on my right side, curling into a ball, and the pain instantly disappeared. I took three long, deep breaths and then it dawned on me that I had to focus on my breathing. As I did so, everything slowed down. *I can do this*, I told myself. *I've been doing it my whole life.* I knew that if I could slow my heart, I would slow the bleeding as well.

I told myself over and over: *Rick, just breathe.*

During the ninety-minute ride to shore, I mostly kept my eyes shut, and drifted in and out of consciousness. Every now and then I would open them and see the puddle of blood in the back of the boat getting larger, and spray from the waves blowing by.

By the time we neared land, I could no longer open my eyes, I couldn't feel my arms or my legs and my heart was barely beating. I was still bleeding; I was dying. But I continued trying to focus on my breath, and as I did, I recalled the many life-and-death events I'd experienced over my diving career and how I'd survived them.

CHAPTER 2

THIS BUD'S FOR YOU

I was walking to my next class in junior high school in Homestead, Florida when I saw an advertisement on the bulletin board for a local spearfishing club. The meeting was on Saturday night, and I couldn't wait to ask my parents if I could join. Their only concern was that the meeting was too far for me to ride my bike—four to five miles—but I assured them I was old enough to do it. My mom said it would be after dark, and she didn't want me on the road after dark.

But my dad simply said, "Well, we better put some lights on that bike." My father never wanted to hold me back from doing or trying anything, and even when things didn't go right, he would pick me up and tell me to try again.

The meeting was being held at the local dive shop, and as I walked into the packed room, a nice lady asked me where my parents were. I told her my parents don't dive, and I wanted to join the club myself. She then asked how I got there, and how I was getting home, and I replied, "On my bicycle." Other adults in the room overheard us, and several asked my age, and I told them I was twelve.

Several of them laughed and said I couldn't join unless I was sponsored. After all, who would take responsibility for a kid? Then I heard a voice boom over all the rest, and he had a strange accent. "Elaine and me. We will sponsor him." The man and woman walked over and introduced themselves as Jon and Elaine. At the end of the evening, Jon put my bike in his car and gave me a ride home.

From the moment I met Jon and Elaine, they treated me like

their very own son. If Jon was going diving on the weekend, he would give me a call, and I would drop everything to get ready and go with him. I had already been spearfishing since I was ten, but Jon made me a much better spearfisherman. He grew up on the Mediterranean, in the former country of Yugoslavia, and was an excellent diver.

One day Jon and Elaine asked if they could come over and meet my parents. During the visit, they said how much they enjoyed my company and said they were going down to the Florida Keys diving and spearfishing for a three-day Club weekend and wanted me to come along. My eyes were wide with excitement and in my head, I was screaming, *Please say yes, please say yes.* And they did.

I was used to being on Jon's boat and knew what to do. I knew how to cast off, tie back up, and work the anchor. Those were my responsibilities. Jon also taught me how to drive the boat just in case I needed to move it in an emergency. Jon taught me how to do things the right way from the very beginning, so there was never any confusion. One of the things that he engrained in me was that the boat, as well as everyone in it, was my responsibility. I would help the guests get dressed and enter the water first, before I would get in, and I would always get out of the water first so I could help them get back into the boat.

My favorite thing to do was chase fish. If a guest shot a fish that got away, I would chase it down just to give it back to them. I was like a bird dog, but with fish. If the guest shot a fish and it slipped into a cave, my job was to dive down and dig it out. Everyone was always astonished at my helpfulness, but I just thought it was fun.

During that first weekend away in the Florida Keys with Jon and Elaine, we were joined by many others from the dive club, and we all stayed at the same hotel near the marina. We dove all day and returned late, and while all the adults walked off the boats to grab a cold drink and sit around the pool to discuss the day and plans for the next day, I went to work. The boat was my responsibility, and I didn't need anyone telling me what to do. It needed to be washed, and after I washed the boat, I washed all the dive gear.

People kept seeing me walk by and placing their washed dive gear up on the drying rack. I remember one man asking Jon if I was his son or nephew, and he said that I was a friend. Then the man asked why he bothered taking me out diving. Jon replied that I was a better diver than any of them, that I never got tired, and that I took care of his boat, as if it were his own. Then he added: "Most of all, he's a good kid."

During the club's first spearfishing competition, Jon had the very best divers in his boat, and they wanted to dive an area of the reef that was very deep. The method used was the boat would put out four lines, and the divers would get dragged behind the boat while it was in gear. They could cover more ground looking for big fish. Then when they saw a fish, they would signal through their snorkel with a honk, then drop the line, dive down and shoot the fish. The depth of water was 65-75 feet which at that time was deeper than I have ever tried to dive.

The event went on for several hours and I stayed with Jon in the boat. Finally, he asked me why I wasn't in the water yet. I told him the water was too deep and I couldn't dive that deep. "Bullshit," he answered and abruptly stopped the boat. "Well, you certainly are not going to shoot any fish sitting in the boat."

The other men gathered around the back of the boat and asked why it had stopped. Jon told them what I said, and they all paused. Jon told one of the men to get out of the water and drive the boat, and then Jon got in with me. He held my hand and told me to take three good breaths slowly, then dive. He and the other men stayed with me on my first dive all the way down to the bottom 75 feet below. When we all came up, they were cheering me on saying, "Not bad at all for a twelve-year-old."

Jon gave me a smile and a wink and said he knew I could do it. The rest of the day Jon would point out fish and watch over me while I dove down and shot them. I had no idea what I was capable of, and of course Jon was beaming with pride that came from being my mentor.

Upon our return to the marina, our smiles quickly vanished when we saw an ambulance at the boat ramp. The EMT's were pulling a man from a boat who was from our club and in the competition. They tried their best to cover him from view, but his blue hands were visible. It was the first dead person I had ever seen. After the boat was tied up, Jon told me to stay put while he and the other men went to find out what happened and if they could lend a hand. It was a very sad moment, as the wife of the man that died came running up and screamed the moment she looked under the sheet. Her whole world changed that very moment. I still didn't know or understand what had happened. How could a person die spearfishing?

The ride home was filled with silence, broken by my questions about what had happened. But Jon didn't answer me, and I realized he had been good friends with the man. When we got back to my house, Jon asked me to sit in the truck while he went in to talk with my parents. They both came out, got me out of the truck and gave me a big hug. They had heard on the radio that a diver from the competition had drowned, and they were terrified it was me.

Later that evening, my mom and dad sat me down and said they no longer wanted me diving because of the dangers involved in it. For the first time in my life I absolutely refused, and said no, I would not quit. My father looked at me and said, "Well then, you better learn as much as you can about diving, so you don't end up breaking our hearts by getting hurt or worse." Right then and there I swore an oath to them both that I would not only learn how to dive safely, but someday they would be very proud of the diver I would become.

Soon after the incident, Jon opened to me about his friend who died that day. He told me he drowned, but I couldn't fathom how that could happen. Then he explained that the man drowned from "shallow water blackout." When I asked what that was, he looked at me and said: "You promise me right now that you will never take more than three breaths, and no fish is ever worth your life!" I could tell Jon meant every word, and I promised.

What was it about "three breaths" and what was shallow water blackout? I wondered. I went to the library and checked out every book on spearfishing I could find, and there it was. In every book there was a dedicated chapter on the dangers of spearfishing, and the number one killer was shallow water blackout.

It's a complicated malady that I found difficult to understand at my age, but all the books underlined how to prevent it, so I focused on that. First rule was to never hyperventilate, and that was why Jon was telling me to take only three slow breaths before making a dive. Next rule is to always give your body time to recover between dives, so you can not only re-oxygenate yourself, but also to get rid of built-up carbon dioxide in your body.

My plan was simple and one that was easy for me to remember. No more than three slow breaths prior to leaving the surface and stay three times longer on the surface between dives than I did on the bottom. If I was down for one minute on the bottom, I would stay at least three minutes on the surface recovering before diving again.

Superbowl Sunday was a big event in our house, and the game in 1974 was no different. My father was a proud Miami Dolphins fan and looking forward to the game. My mom scrambled around the kitchen making snacks and getting everyone drinks while my dad sat like the king of the house in his favorite chair as the game against the Minnesota Vikings got underway. That day would also be the day that defined the rest of my life. I liked football, but the best part of the Superbowl Sunday has always been halftime. Cheerleaders on the field, rock stars singing, and of course the commercials.

This particular year Budweiser Beer had a "This Bud's for You" commercial for Navy divers, and it featured two Navy divers using a rock drill, to pull core samples from the ocean floor. I jumped up, popcorn went flying everywhere, and I exclaimed, "I am going to do that!"

My mom said, "No way!" But my dad just gave me a smile and said, "I bet you will."

Now I was on a mission. I was going to be a Navy diver and I had five years to get ready. I asked my dad, who was a retired Air Force master sergeant, to take me to the Navy recruiter because I wanted to ask some questions. At first, he said I was way too young, and I would probably change my mind as I got older. But I was determined.

After relentlessly asking my father to take me, he finally agreed and walked me into the recruiter's office. The recruiter happened to be a frogman, and a member of the Navy's underwater demolition team. My father told him I wanted to be a Navy diver and the recruiter asked, "Why not a Frogman?"

Neither my father nor I understood the difference between the two, and the frogman did his best to explain: Navy divers work underwater, and Navy frogmen use the water as a method to get ashore and do covert operations, just as they might parachute out of planes to get to their intended target.

I still did not understand the difference so the recruiter broke it down even simpler. "Young man, do you think you could kill someone?" My father and I looked at each other and both of us said, "No!" at the same time.

"Then you want to be a Navy diver, not a frogman," the recruiter said, then gave me a copy of the physical fitness test. Navy frogmen, who are now called SEALS, take a fitness test called BUDS, which stands for Basic Under Water Demolition School. The frogman explained, "The Navy dive school fitness test and BUDS are the same."

If I could work on one thing, it would be the challenges in that fitness test. He told me not to take that test lightly, that seventy-five percent of highly fit men fail it on induction.

As I moved into my mid-teens, I was expected to get a job. Finding one wouldn't be a problem, except I wanted one where I wouldn't have to work on weekends, so I could go spearfishing. Just then our school started a program, called "work experience," that allowed me to go to school just three hours a day from 7:00 to 10:00 am. Then I could work from 10:30 to 5:30 pm Monday through Friday. This was perfect as it allowed for me to have the weekends off to continue spearfishing, and I was working a full-time job while going to school.

If it wasn't tough enough for me keeping my mom from freaking out every time I was out diving, in 1975 the movie *JAWS* landed in every movie theatre around the globe. My mom went bonkers after watching the movie, which also scared the wits out of my little sister. To this day, she still cannot put one toe in the ocean. But the movie did not phase me one bit.

Mom demanded that my father put a halt to me diving on the weekend, but fortunately my father wouldn't hear of it. In fact, my father promoted my diving by helping me find my first boat at age fourteen. I was working full time and had more than enough money to buy a nice sixteen-foot runabout boat. Despite my mom's constant protests, my father took me down to the boat ramp with friends on the weekend, and dropped me off, telling me he'd be back at 5 pm. "And don't be late," he would say.

I knew my passion for diving was putting a great divide between my parents, and I loved my father dearly for protecting me and my passion. Sure, my dad was not a waterman, nor did he ever go diving with me. But he taught me more about being a man than anyone. I watched my father working two and sometimes three jobs to give us a better life, only to come home and hear my mom upset, complaining about me diving somewhere.

Prior to going into the Navy, I stayed busy between school, full time work, working out, and diving on the weekends. I could not stand to be at home and hear them argue, and I wanted to leave as soon as it was possible. I graduated high school early and asked them both to sign for me, so I could enlist in the Navy at age seventeen.

Bootcamp was an absolute blast for me, and it was very much like my upbringing. I was expected at home to make my own bed, wash and fold my own clothes, and keep my room tidy, and the Navy expected the same thing. When someone messed up, we would all get punished. Again, it was just like at home. I shared a room with my two older brothers and if the room was messy, we all paid the price of my mother's wrath. The only difference was the punishment in bootcamp was usually pushups, but I had been doing pushups for five years. It all was nothing more than a game to me and I breezed right through with a smile on my face.

Upon graduation from bootcamp, I was allowed to go home to see my family. My father picked me up alone at the airport and for the first time in my life he said to me, "Let's get a drink at the bar." I thought it was because I graduated, but it was a speech that parents hate giving their children. Dad and Mom were getting a divorce. I didn't say a word because deep down I knew it was for the best. When we got home, I asked if I could go pick my sister up from school.

After dropping her at home, I drove down to Key West and cried the whole way. I spent the night in a hotel before returning home the next day. For the rest of my stay, I was numb and didn't want to be there. I couldn't wait to go to my next duty station, which was in Chicago. It seemed like my friends were all doing the same dumb shit from high school, but I had moved ahead and wanted more in my life. I no longer fit in and now I felt like an outsider. But then it dawned on me that I had a new family, the Navy.

It was the last time I would ever go home to visit my family.

CHAPTER 3

DEAL IS A DEAL

I arrived at Great Lakes Naval Base just outside of Chicago in September of 1979. Back then, a recruit couldn't go directly into the Navy dive school because the Navy wanted all sailors to be trained in a specific field first. That way, should you get hurt or drop out of training, you would have a job to fall back on. At first, I was told that I would become an engineman and be trained to work on diesel engines. Since that was one of the source ratings to become a Navy diver, that was fine with me. However, the Navy needed mechanics for the new gas turbine powered destroyers. So, when I got to Great Lakes, I was reclassified from engineman to gas turbine specialist.

It didn't matter to me. I just wanted to get into diving school as soon as I could. I kept asking, if I do this training, will I be allowed to become a Navy diver? The classifier assured me yes, I could. I even went so far as to ask my chief and the officer in charge, and they, too, assured me I could, and I would be able to go to Navy dive school. I would later find out after I was assigned to my first ship, that they had all lied to me under the guise that the needs of the Navy outweighed my personal desires.

I plodded my way through the gas turbine mechanical school and graduated in the spring after a long cold winter at Great Lakes. Finally, my orders came for me to be transferred to a new gas turbine powered destroyer called the USS *Stump*. The ship was on a Mediterranean cruise and I needed to catch up with it during a port call. Along with those orders came a plane ticket on a commercial jet to Madrid. From there, I was told to take a bus or train to Rota Naval Base, Spain.

That may sound easy, but I was only eighteen years old, and was flying to Europe by myself. I called my dad and told him the news. He was shocked the Navy would put a kid on such an international travel itinerary by himself. "You can do this, Rick," he said. "Just keep your head down and speak to no one. Always look like you know what you're doing and where you're going, just like you've done it in the past."

I boarded the flight from New York to Madrid, and I must have looked incredibly young, because the flight attendant asked if I was traveling alone or with my parents. I proudly told her I was a third-class petty officer in the Navy going to my first ship. She said, "Bless your heart," and moved me to first class. I landed in Madrid, found a train, and got down to Rota Naval Base, only to be told that my ship wasn't there. It was in Sicily. I was given another plane ticket, and the next day I landed in Sicily. But again, I was told my ship wasn't there.

After staying in Sicily more than a week, I was ordered to go to the military airport where I would catch a plane for Nice, France. I hustled over to the assigned runway, but there wasn't a single plane in sight. As I stood there looking at the empty tarmac, a Leer Jet swooped down, and the door opened. The 6th Fleet chief of staff stepped out for a stretch and said to me, "Young man, your chariot awaits."

Once inside, the chief of staff said the Navy was worried about me and had begun a search for my whereabouts. He apologized for his staff sending me all over Europe and traveling alone. I told him the advice my father gave me to which he replied, "Your father is a smart man." Later that day I reported aboard my ship with my new friend, the 6th Fleet chief of staff. He personally made it a point to ask my commander to take good care of me.

Upon checking in, I was told my ship was on its third month into a six-month deployment and we would be traveling throughout the Mediterranean. Then we would cross the Atlantic back to our home port in Norfolk, Virginia. I politely asked when I would be allowed to go to Navy dive school, and was told that wasn't possible, nor would it ever be possible, since there was a critical shortage of gas turbine mechanics.

I told my chief this was a big mistake, and that the only reason I entered the Navy was to become a diver. He replied that nothing could be done. For the first time in my life, I wanted to quit. I felt trapped and every day that passed, I went into a deeper and deeper depression. Throughout the remainder of the cruise, I focused on getting qualified on as many things as I could before the ship returned to Norfolk and I qualified as an engineering top watch.

Once back in Norfolk, we were supposed to stand down, which meant we would be off duty for a few months. However, the captain called us all together and said our ship was heading out again. He explained another ship could not make its scheduled Unitas cruise—sea exercises involving several countries—around South America, so we were taking its place. The captain was quite excited to tell us all that we were to be the Flag ship for the commodore during this cruise, which meant the commodore would be staying onboard our ship during the entire cruise.

I was thinking, great another six to eight months away from home port. How was I ever to get to dive school? The Navy dive school was just twenty miles away at Little Creek Amphibious Base in Virginia Beach, so I decided to go speak to someone there. I needed to find out for myself if anything could be done, or if I was doomed to spend the next six years as an engineer aboard a destroyer. I got an interview with a senior chief diver and told him my story. As soon as he found out I would be leaving shortly on another cruise, he handed me all the required paperwork to apply for the school. He told me to come and see him when I got back, and he would see if there was anything he could do.

I went back to my ship and was sitting on my rack (bed) holding all the paperwork when I came up with a plan. I figured I had absolutely nothing to lose. The worse thing they could do to me was send me to the brig, but I felt I was already in jail, trapped doing something I was never meant to do.

I filled out all the paperwork to the best of my ability, then carefully forged my captain's signature. Next, I asked a friend if I could borrow his summer white jumper uniform. He asked why and I told him it was best if he didn't know. His answer was yes, if I took his duty that Sunday. He was married and wanted to spend as much time with his family before we left for South America. Although I didn't want to take his duty, I needed his jumper.

His rating was GMM3, which was Gunner's Mate Missiles, and that was another source rating for Navy diver school. My rate, GSM3 Gas Turbine Mechanical, was not a source rating, so I was hoping no one would notice the difference in the one letter. I asked my chief for the following day off and jumped on my motorcycle and rode to Washington DC.

Driving up to the Pentagon, I was as nervous as a cornered cat and after I parked, I went through several security checkpoints. As I entered the building, my heart was pounding, my face was flushed, and I could not believe what I was about to do. But nothing was going to stop me from becoming a Navy diver. Looking for the Navy diver detailer in a building that was twenty-eight acres and five stories tall is a bigger task than finding a sugar crystal in a saltshaker. But lucky for me someone recognized I was lost and knew exactly where to take me. The sign on the door said, Master Chief/Master Diver Detailer, so I knocked loudly and stepped in. Even though the master chief had his back to me, I could tell he was covered in tattoos, and I noticed the name plate on his desk said, Mad Dog.

He spun around in his chair and looked like a Hell's Angel biker. "What can I do for you, son?" I introduced myself as GMM3 Bettua and told him I wanted to be a Navy diver, then handed him the 1306 form that I signed for my captain, and the other required forms. He looked at me and asked me two questions. "Have you completely qualified for all your duties onboard the USS *Stump*"? I answered that I had. Then he asked, "Do you have Captain's backing"?

At that moment I thought I was caught, my hands instantly started to sweat and I couldn't speak. The master chief then said, "You seem like a pretty good kid, I'm surprised he's willing to let you go. Okay, Petty Officer Bettua, I will screen your qualifications and if I think you're what we're looking for, I will let you know."

The USS *Stump* was heading south in a flotilla of ten ships with the Commodore onboard. The Unitas cruise promotes the U.S. around all the South American countries and the island nations in the Caribbean. After visiting Trinidad and Tobago, the task force then traveled south stopping in every country along the way. Then after rounding the southern tip of South America, we moved up the West Coast, and finally passed through the Panama Canal en route back to Norfolk.

Life onboard a Navy ship is not that much different from civilian life. The first few days underway are a bit stressful and nothing goes smoothly, but then everyone gets into a routine, and before you know it the ship and crew are in rhythm. But I was uneasy. After all, I'd lied to the master diver. Well, I lied about a few things, but one cut much deeper. The master chief asked if I was fully qualified onboard and I said yes, but that was not quite right. I had been holding back on my final damage control qualifications, maybe because I resented being lied to about Navy diver school. But now I had to make up for it and went to my chief and told him I was ready.

Being part of the damage control party at sea is no joke. In the event of a fire, flooding or even a missile attack at sea, your job is to save the ship and the crew. One of the most demanding jobs is the fast reaction team. These guys rush head-first into the problem area once an emergency is reported. If a fire breaks out, they quickly handle it, if it's small. But if the fire is too large to easily put out, they get dressed out as the #1 and #2 nozzleman and fight the fire. I was made for that job as I was lightning quick, and small enough to race through the ship and hatches, barely slowing down.

I was also fearless, and it was a game to me, much like chasing fish when I was younger. My partner and I practiced relentlessly, racing to the scene to see who could get there first. The alarm went off announcing, "This is a Drill. This is a Drill. Fire, Fire, Fire, Class Bravo Fire," then the location was given. Everyone on board knew to stand back when the quick reaction team raced across the 510-foot-long ship to the location of the "fire."

Nothing can ever prepare you for the moment the emergency is real. For several days, the seas were rough and the ship was pitching back and forth, and most of the crew were seasick. I was in my rack trying my best not to get sick when the alarm went off.

Fire, Fire, Fire Class Bravo, Fire! Aft Steering!

This time there was no message saying that it was a drill. I bolted for the location knowing already that it wasn't going to be a small fire.

There are three classes of fires at sea, Alpha which stands for ash. This is easy to put out with a CO_2 extinguisher or water. Class C is an electrical fire, one where we shut down the power source and use CO_2 to extinguish. Class Bravo is a killer, and it is either fuel or oil, and very difficult to put out. The heat intensity is much greater and requires a blanket of foam over the oil or fuel to cool and smother it.

My partner and I arrived at the same time at aft steering, and the watertight door was warm to the touch. As I opened it, I noticed the fire in the back section of the compartment. My partner entered the space with a CO_2 extinguisher, and within seconds went down to his knees, and dropped the extinguisher. It dawned on me something was wrong with the air, or there was a lack of oxygen from the fire raging.

I held my breathe while I grabbed him with two hands around his collar and dragged him out. Once outside the aft steering compartment, I slammed and secured the door, before finally taking a breath. My partner quickly recovered and raced back to dress out for the number two nozzleman position. This time when we re-entered the space, we had a team behind us, and we had compressed air tanks to help us breathe.

We fought the fire until it was out. There was no time to ease up or take a break, not until we were certain that it was out. After it was over, and we were relaxing outside on the upper deck, the captain and commodore came over and said, "Good Job." Then the commodore asked my name and said, "My god, son. How old are you?" I answered his questions with a big smile on my dirty face. For the rest of my time during that cruise the commodore remembered my name, and he would go out of his way to check on me.

I also felt good that I'd made up for my lie to the master diver at the Pentagon. I now had all my qualifications. At this point, I couldn't do anything more to get into dive school. For the rest of the cruise, I just wanted to be the best asset aboard our ship.

In some ways, the Navy is the easiest job in the world. They tell you exactly what you need to do, and then after you do it, they reward you. I noticed the moment I got fully qualified onboard everything instantly got easier. There was no pressure or stress, and in my free time I could do what I liked, which usually included working out and running as much as possible.

Many sailors complained and dragged their feet getting qualified, and many never get qualified at all. But those sailors never got anywhere and blamed the system for their own inabilities. I didn't hang around negative people, and all I knew was I was enjoying my new-found popularity. It was as if I'd become the ship's mascot. After all, of the four hundred sailors aboard, I was the youngest, and it seemed that everyone from the cooks to the quartermasters, wanted to look after me. Even going out in foreign ports I was never alone; the older guys always watched over me and ensured my safety like a bunch of older brothers.

Every enlisted man onboard that ship knew I wanted to be a Navy diver, and although the officers didn't want to admit it, they knew it was only a matter of time before I figured it out. At each port we visited, once my duties were complete, I walked off the ship and went running. This was back in 1980 when running was not a very popular sport. Sailors sat on the ship and watched me on the pier, doing pushups and sit-ups until I was too exhausted to do another one.

To many of them, I think I represented something they hoped they had in themselves –unwavering perseverance. All of them wanted me to become a Navy diver and went out of their way to secretly help. The ship's welding supervisor asked if I needed anything and if he could help, and I said I need a pull up bar. The very next day he welded 6 pull up bars around the ship so I could do as many as possible. Other sailors would get on bikes and motivate me while I was running, which always just made me laugh. But everyone it seemed was helping me achieve my goal, and I was thankful.

Late one evening while pulling into Rio de Janeiro, Brazil, the captain stopped the ship outside the harbor. He got on the ship's 1MC (microphone) and asked us all to step out onto the main deck and look at something amazing. It was dark and up in the sky was a massive illuminated cross. He went on to say the cross was a statue of "Christ the Redeemer" that was more than one-hundred-feet high, and it was perched atop of a massive mountain.

When I looked up at the statue, tears welled in my eyes and the name, "Christ the Redeemer," echoed in my head like a chant. I knew my time was now, and that I would have help from a higher source. Later that night I could not sleep, and all night long I tossed and turned. I knew a storm was fast approaching.

The next day started out like any other, right up to the point where the captain himself came back on the 1MC and said, "Petty Officer Bettua, my cabin now!" The only time the captain used the 1MC was to speak to the entire crew, and he never used it for anything else. The fact that he was now ordering me to his cabin was a testament that I was in grave trouble.

I ran as fast as I could up four flights of stairs and every time I passed another sailor, they looked at me as if it was the last time I would ever be seen. I knocked at his door, entered, and announced myself, "Petty Officer Bettua, Sir," and stood at attention. The commodore was also in the room standing behind the captain, who was clearly angry, his face crimson with fury. He abruptly shouted, "I want to know how you did this!"

I caught my breath. "Did what, Sir?"

"Don't get smart with me!" he steamed. "You know damn well what I'm talking about. I want to know why I am holding a set of orders for you to go to Navy dive school and I have no idea about them!"

The captain was very intimidating, and I was nothing more than a teenager. I couldn't speak and I was blinking away tears while he demanded once again that I explain how these orders came about.

Finally, the commodore broke the silence and calmly said, "Petty Officer Bettua just tell your captain how you did it."

Suddenly, six years of emotions started running out of my mouth starting with the 1974 Super Bowl Sunday and the "This Bud's for You Navy Divers" commercial. Then the years of training and staying focused and true to my dream of one day becoming one.

The captain rubbed his face with both hands, ready to explode, and the commodore said again, "Son, just tell him."

So, I did. "Sir, I took all the paperwork and signed your name to it, got on my motorcycle and delivered it personally to the master chief/master diver detailer in Washington, D.C."

The room fell silent for way too long, and it was looking like I would have to accept my fate. Just then the commodore started laughing, and the captain himself soon followed in and said to me, "Well, if you're not cheating, you're not trying hard enough."

I didn't know whether to cry or laugh, so I stood completely quiet.

To my amazement, the captain stood and said he would be sorry for losing one of his best sailors, but he understood my drive to become a diver. He then said, "By the looks of your orders, you will graduate just prior to our return to Norfolk, Virginia."

He grabbed my hand firmly, looked into my eyes and said, "You will be on the pier in uniform with that dive pin on your chest when we pull in. You will tie up the ship's number #1 line and salute me on the bridge. Do you understand?"

I said, "Yes sir!"

And the last thing he said was: "Petty Officer Bettua, don't you forget. A deal is a deal. Don't you ever quit"

"No, sir, not a chance!"

CHAPTER 4

UNLEASH HIM

The ship stayed in Rio de Janeiro about a week before finally sailing off. But it left without me. I cast off all the lines and then saluted all the officers and chiefs before running down the pier and waving goodbye to all my shipmates. I was the underdog, and at that time I represented every enlisted sailor on that ship who had a dream. It was a long shot back in those days, and everyone was shouting at me and wishing me good luck.

In those days if one hundred very fit young men tried out for the dive program, seventy-five would fail the physical fitness exam. Of those twenty-five who continued, a dozen at best would graduate, but I was very focused and looking forward to the next challenge in my life.

I landed in Norfolk, Virginia on a Thursday afternoon and my plan was simple. I would stay at the airport hotel overnight, and the following morning catch a taxi to my storage facility to get my motorcycle, then drive over to Little Creek Naval Amphibious Base and check into dive school. I awoke early and got my uniform ready, still using my friend's dress white jumper with the GMM3 rating badge.

I took my time as I had all day to check into dive school. It also happened to be a three-day weekend, so we would not be starting class until the following Tuesday. After grabbing my motorcycle, I headed onto the base, and everything was going as well as could be expected. I could see the dive school half a mile down the road, and I must have had the biggest grin from ear to ear under my helmet. I was finally going to get there after six years of preparations.

In a fraction of a second, that all changed as disaster struck. A car failed to stop at the intersection and plowed into me. My GS-1100 Suzuki slammed to the pavement and skidded off the road. The peg stuck in the asphalt, flipping the bike on top of me.

I lay there under a motorcycle that was three times my weight. I was in shock, bloody and bruised. People rushed over and pulled the bike off me and helped me up. Not only was my borrowed uniform shredded from the road rash, but I was bleeding from my arms and legs. Then I felt the pain in my chest. It hurt while inhaling, and that would certainly be a disqualifier. The lady who ran the intersection was crying, and tried to call the base police and ambulance, but I stopped her. I told her I was fine and not to worry.

"What about your motorcycle?" she asked.

It didn't matter, I told her. I was getting rid of it. I was injured, and in pain, but needed to get away, before an ambulance took me away to the hospital. People helped me get on my bike and I drove away. I pulled up to the dive school that afternoon, and fortunately not many people were around. I cleaned myself up a bit, walked onto the quarterdeck, handed my orders to the officer of the deck, and said I was reporting for dive school. The officer was a young ensign and she asked me what happened. I told her I was in an accident but assured her I was fine. She just looked at me and said, "You have three days to get ready, good luck."

I drove back to my storage shed to assess the damage and started to remove my uniform. I had road rash and cuts on both arms, and my left knee was cut up. But the worst of it was the sharp pain I felt when I inhaled deeply. I changed into my civilian clothes and drove to Roanoke, where I went to the hospital. I wanted to be as far away from the base as possible so no one there would know I was injured.

An emergency room nurse cleaned me up, exposing the road rash and treating it. An ER doctor walked in and ordered a chest x-ray. The pain in my chest was even worse now. There was redness and swelling on my lower right rib cage where the bike had flipped on top of me. The doctor examined the x-ray and exclaimed that there was good news and bad news. He said I would live, but that I had fractured two ribs that were going to be quite sore for the next four to six weeks.

This news was unfathomable to me, and I told the doctor I had been waiting six years to go to Navy dive school, and if I couldn't pass the physical fitness test on Tuesday morning, my career would be over. He asked what I needed to do, and I explained the test to him. At first, he said that would be impossible, but then he saw the desperation in my eyes. "Listen young man, there is nothing preventing you from doing what you need to do besides the pain you're going to feel."

He told me that as I did those exercises, my ribs will flex and cause a great deal of discomfort. He added that he doubted that I could hurt myself worse. It was just the pain that I would have to endure. Then he added that he would prescribe something that would take the edge off the pain. "When the pain comes, and it will, I want you to ignore it and push through. If you are as tough as I think you are, you will get through fine."

He told me to take it easy for the next three days and wished me luck. That weekend I stayed at a Roanoke motel where I focused on light stretching and breathing. With each passing day, the pain was getting less intense, but I knew it would return.

Tuesday morning, we all reported for duty and the instructors went over the rules and correct method for doing each exercise. This PT Test consisted of a 500-yard swim (breaststroke or side stroke) in less than ten minutes, then fifty-two perfect pushups going all the way down to the ground, fifty-two sit ups with no one holding your legs, then eight chin ups palms away and no jerking. That would be followed by a 1.5 mile run in less than ten minutes.

There was no part of this test that was not going to hurt, or so I told myself. One hundred sailors were competing for a spot in school. I was not my usual self; the drugs the doctor had given me made me feel off. I was quiet, and I kept to myself. I told myself, *Rick, you got this, you have been doing this PT test for six years.* Even though I was hurt, I was certain that I would be better than most of the men in the crowd.

The swim test was first, and normally I swim breaststroke. But that was out of the question now, so I switched to side stroke on my unaffected side and swam the distance in 9:15. Push-ups were a breeze, and so were the sit-ups. Then the instructor told me to mount the pull up bar. I jumped up, and my full weight stretched my chest. It hurt so bad I wanted to scream, but I bit my tongue, and just told myself to breathe instead. Once off the bar I knew I was home free, and my run time was 8:50. I not only passed, but I was in the top 10% of my class.

When the day was done, we ended up with only sixteen sailors to start the course. We all heard rumors from the instructors, that was not enough to convene a class, and we all might be held over for the next class in spring. But the following morning, a van arrived with nine frogmen, an underwater demolition team, and that brought us up to twenty-five.

Back in 1980, there was no war going on and so the UDTs were being under-utilized. So, they volunteered to go through the Navy Deep Sea Dive School to hone their diving skills. I was surprised that most of them were about my size or slightly bigger, and they were all in great shape.

It was as if these guys had a full-time job just working out. You could tell their confidence level was high as each stepped out of the van. Instead of them grouping together, they walked through our ranks, and politely introduced themselves, and shook our hands, which put us all at ease. Then they seamlessly mixed into our group, and we all formed one team. The motto for frogman in those days was "silent professionals," and these guys exemplified that. They knew the true meaning of teamwork.

I loved everything about dive school: the working out, learning to dive, even classwork and especially the comradery. The frogs made everything fun, and they made everything look easy. None of them were intimidated by the instructors and many times they were the glue that kept us all together. One of them, a guy named Art, was not much older than me, and we began a friendship that would span our entire careers. We were the youngest in the class, and we stuck close together. He helped me with the physical fitness challenges, and I helped him in the classroom.

On the weekends, we would run or swim together and study. One weekend Art and I decided to run down to the beach with our fins and go for a long swim along the miles of empty beach. We had a swim test coming up, so we wanted to make sure we were ready. We swam for miles and the whole time I was talking to my friend.

Finally, Art motioned toward the beach, and we sat in the surf and he asked me where I had learned to swim like that. I told him I grew up in south Florida chasing fish. He replied, "Rick, you are a fish." Then he asked me why I didn't want to become a frogman. I told him I didn't want to have to kill anybody, and he said he didn't either.

It was getting cold in Little Creek and ice started to form on the bay. One of our timed challenges was a thousand-yard swim with fins on, and the sheets of ice on the bay would not make it easy. We were all paired up with a short line connecting each swimmer, and we were freezing our butts off, when they finally said go. I swam as fast as my partner could, and the whole way encouraged him to go that much faster.

When the test was over, there was no surprise that all the frogs were all faster than the sailors. The master chief /master diver in charge of the school had been in the Navy more than three decades. He was a large man with a short temper. The longer he watched the test, the angrier he got. Sure, the frogs were snickering a little bit, but the master chief had a soft spot for us divers and called all the instructors over.

I overheard the conversation because the master chief's voice was loud. "Are you telling me we don't have one sailor boy who can keep up with them frogs?" One instructor spoke up. "Maybe Bettua."

The master chief spun around, scanned the gathered divers, then ordered me front and center. I unsnapped the line between me and my swim buddy, and ran over. "Yes, Master Chief."

"Bettua, can you beat these frogs?"

"Yes, Master Chief," I replied without hesitating. "I just ask one thing. I want to use the same fins that they have on."

He nodded. "Fair enough."

The following morning as we all put on our heavy-duty

wetsuits, the frogs were looking at me as they knew I posed a challenge. The master chief asked if we had any teams of three and was told we did. He said, "Make them a pair and let Bettua swim alone. I want to see something." With that, I was unleashed.

As we were about to start the race, the master chief glanced over at me, then shouted, "Go!" and we were off. Just like chasing fish in the warm water off Florida, go means go, and there were at least eight frogs whose mission was to show me they were faster. Crossing the finish line, I could see they were all well behind me and I could see the master chief was beaming with pride.

After all of us exited the water, a few of the frogs were mumbling under their breath, and the master chief walked up to them and asked if they had something to say. Several said the swim was not fair because Bettua was unleashed. The master chief smiled and said, "You think that makes a difference. Well, let's find out right now."

He said, "Unleash the frogs," but my friend Art protested, and said he didn't want anything to do with this test. "Master Chief, I already know Bettua can beat me."

"Fair enough," the master chief replied, then demanded the other eight frogs and I get back into the frigid water. I never wanted to be put in a position where I felt what I was doing was a competition, but for whatever reason, I was chosen to make a statement.

All of us were at the ready when the master chief glanced over at me, and the look on his face told me to win. When he said go, I was gone and did the first fifty yards underwater. I heard the master chief shout, "Where did Bettua go?" But then I popped up well ahead of the others, and the whole way increased the distance with every kick. What surprised me most was after we all exited the water, each frog humbly came up to me and said, "Good job, Ricky."

That was the day I knew I had a gift, and that gift was swimming.

The last part of our training was called Mark V, and it involved the wearing of the old heavy copper and brass helmets. It's what more people associate with deep sea divers. The helmets at that time had been around for the last fifty years and were the cornerstone for all deep-sea diving since before World War II. The suit itself weighed about two hundred and five pounds, and I weighed one hundred and fifty-five pounds.

Art and I were sent to get some equipment and while picking it up, we ran into a second-class diver who had just graduated in the class before us. He told us both a few secrets to help us get through training, and then said, "Watch out for the moving out exercise in Mark V." He told us that the whole class failed, and he believed the instructors had it rigged so that would happen. The exercise was not difficult on paper or so it seemed. It consisted of MK-V diving gear, walking down a ladder to the bottom of the bay, and moving out fifty yards to a buoy. Once you got to the buoy, you would pull it down signaling you found it. Easy, but the diver said when we got to the bottom, we would sink in the mud up to our waist and there was absolutely no visibility to move out and find the buoy.

Art and I sat around one Friday night having a beer thinking of ways we could get the class to pass this test, which was to commence Monday morning. Then I said, "I know what we do. How about you and I dive this weekend and attach a heavy line from the bottom of the ladder out to the buoy. Then when the divers get to the bottom, they can grab the line, and pull themselves out to the buoy." I had been scuba diving since I was thirteen and since Art was a frogman, he was qualified as well.

No one was around the school on the weekends, especially Sunday mornings, so we quietly timed our arrival for sunrise. The dive school and dive staging area were built on a pontoon, so it was very easy for us to get the gear and slip into the water. Once in the water with the line, we headed down. As we'd been told, the visibility was poor, and once we got to the bottom, the mud got stirred up. We tied one end to the bottom rung of the ladder and swam out looking for the buoy. The water was dark, but Art was right next to me, so I pushed on. Just when it looked like we might not find it, the buoy rope was silhouetted by the sunrise. We attached the line to the heavy weight marking the buoy and we were done.

No one saw us do it.

Sunday night we got the class together and told them all about the exercise and what we had done. Art and I were proud of ourselves as the two youngest students in the class taking the initiative to rig the exercise for everyone. All the older frogs smiled and chimed in, "Brass balls," one said. "Well, if you're not cheating, you're not trying hard enough," another said, and "Good job, boys." I made a point to tell everyone when pulling themselves out to the buoy, to zig zag a bit, so the instructors would not get wise that we had a line on the bottom. We all laughed and looked forward to the next day.

Aside from the master diver, we had several instructors, who were either first-class divers or diving medical technicians. One of the instructors was a first-class petty officer and first-class diver, and he was an absolute prick to us sailors. He would punish us every opportunity he got, while looking over at the frogmen for approval, which never came. They didn't respect him or his leadership style, and they said many times he was a bad example and a bully. That Monday one by one we were all dressed out in Mark V and had a turn at the project.

We all laughed to ourselves as some divers exaggerated the zig zags on the bottom but would finally pull the buoy down like a blind mouse. The last diver of the day totally forgot what we all went over the night before and hit the bottom and moved out straight to the buoy and signaled it in less than a minute. The instructor immediately called bullshit, and when the diver came up, he suited up in scuba gear to go down and check the area and found the line.

The instructors were angry and had us all in the pushup position for at least twenty minutes on the quay wall, while they tried to figure which of us was involved. The instructor who was a bully was leading the charge, and walked over to me and said, "You probably did it, you little shit". My silence only enraged him, so he kicked me in the ribs as hard as he could, which were fractured only a few months before. Everyone in the class and all the instructors knew I had an accident the day I reported to school, and they all knew my ribs were fractured. His kick lifted me three feet in the air, and everyone heard me gasp in pain. Before he could kick me again, I admitted I did it. Then one by one the frogs got up and grabbed the instructor, while my friend Art ran over to check on me. I thought the frogs were about to kill the bully. Chiefs and officers from the school charged out to break up what would have been a slaughter.

All of us stood at attention for what seemed like hours. I heard instructors demanding my disenrollment. Several chiefs came out, and asked me who helped me, and specifically who dove with me, but I remained silent. Then an old truck pulled up and it was the master chief, who must've had a few days off. As he walked by to his office, he looked at us all like we were in trouble.

I stood near the door at attention and could hear every word while the instructor who kicked me explained the situation to the master chief. But he said nothing about hurting me. The master chief was clearly aggravated. "So, what do you want me to do?"

"Drop Bettua from training."

"Are you fucking kidding me?" he shouted. "I love that boy and he is the honor man of the class. He ain't going nowhere!"

The master chief then ordered me into his office "front and center," and asked me why I did it.

"So everyone would pass," I answered.

"So, you did it for your classmates?"

"Yes, sir."

The master chief then turned his attention to the instructor. "You're only mad because he outsmarted you."

Then there was a knock at the door, and it was the most senior frogman, a first-class petty officer, and he asked for permission to speak. The master chief told him to go ahead, and he explained how the instructor had kicked me in my previously fractured ribs, and that was what caused the outbreak. Even while going through the physical tests, you could be punished. But an instructor could not put his hands on you with malice.

The master chief stood up and looked at his instructor. "You're fired. Now get the fuck out of my sight!"

After the instructor left, the master chief said. "I think that's enough drama for the day." He asked me to follow him, so we walked out onto the far end of the quay wall, where he stopped and turned to me. "You know, I've got to punish you."

"Yes, sir."

He told me my class standings were the highest, and if I stayed on track, I would be the class honor man. But he was going to take that away from me. I didn't care because I never knew class honor man even existed, so I just smiled and said, "Roger that, Master Chief."

The last day at dive school all of us divers got the chance to speak on the phone to the Navy's highest-ranking diver, master chief/master diver detailer at the Pentagon to receive our orders. Since I'd met him in person, I had a clear image of him, the tattoos and image of a Hell's Angel biker. The way it worked was you would speak to him in the order of your class standings. So, the class honor man would get his choice of orders, and it would descend accordingly.

Due to my little clandestine scheme tying a line from the ladder to the buoy, I was in the number two position. I was a bit nervous when I was handed the phone because I didn't know if the master chief knew that I'd cheated on my application, signing my captain's signature. The master chief greeted me with GMM3 Bettua and I said, "No, Master Chief, I'm GSM3 Bettua."

I'd barely gotten the words out, when he went on a rampage, shouting and cussing at me so loud I could barely understand him. But the gist of the one-way conversation was, he knew he was scammed by an eighteen-year-old boy. Then he said to me, "Boy, I don't care how you got there, but you are going to change your rate to a diver's source rating asap."

"Yes, Master Chief."

CHAPTER 5

WATCH THE TIDE

My first duty station as a diver was on the USS *Sierra* AD-18, which was moored to a pier on the west bank of the Cooper River near Charleston, South Carolina. The *Sierra* was a floating repair facility that serviced ships and was about six hundred feet long and at least five stories high.

There were over five hundred men stationed onboard and when I arrived, they added another two hundred women. How good was this for my first duty station? My two favorite things, I thought to myself, diving, and girls—lots of girls! It wasn't hard for the divers to stand out among the other five hundred men. Everyone else wore the standard navy-blue uniform, and only the eight divers wore dark green fatigues. So, every woman on the ship knew who we were.

But diving consumed my life. The Cooper River was notorious for swift currents, massive tides, and brown muddy water. At first, it was extremely difficult working under the ship in totally blacked out conditions caused by muddy water and the lack of light under the ship. To find a location on the bottom side of the ship that needed maintenance, we would have someone inside the ship strike the hull where we needed to work. We literally located sites by using our ears instead of our eyes.

I was getting disorientated and frustrated by this method until a dive-friend, Bib, told me to slow down, relax, and close my eyes. "Now, follow the noise and vibrations to the job site." That worked. He also said that if I felt disoriented, I should watch my bubbles, because they always go up toward the surface, not to the side, and not down. So that was like a compass.

I was the duty diver one weekend, which entailed me remaining onboard for those forty-eight hours and staying out of trouble. If an emergency dive job came up, I would call in the other seven divers on our team.

On Saturday evening, I was summoned to the wardroom, which is the commissioned officers' mess, and walked into a meeting of several senior officers and agents from Naval Criminal Investigation Service (NCIS). The ship's executive officer (XO) called me over and said, "Petty Officer Bettua, recall your dive team."

"Yes, sir. What is the job?"

One of the NCIS agents explained that an eighteen-year-old sailor onboard was raped and the sailor who may have committed the crime was seen throwing something in the water. "I need you to dive to see if you can find what was thrown off the ship. We think it was a package that contained the suspect's clothes and possibly a knife."

When I asked where it was thrown, I was told it was in the basin between our ship and the adjacent one that was fifty yards away. I explained that the basin was fifty feet deep, the current was raging, and the visibility was zero. The final ten feet is like thick soup and the bottom is mud. "Lastly, sir, the bottom is littered with old debris this ship has been throwing off for decades. This task will be greater than finding a needle in a haystack and will be very hazardous."

"Petty Officer Bettua, don't you think we owe it to the victim to give it a try?" the XO asked.

"Yes, sir," I replied.

The dive team arrived near midnight, and I briefed them on the job. Their first reaction was to ask if I was diving. I just nodded. I wanted to get the dive boat as close to where the object was thrown. To do so, I asked the sailor who saw the suspect throw the object to stand on the same deck and the same approximate spot with a handheld radio. I told him to radio down to us when we were in the approximate spot where the package landed. We maneuvered the dive boat out into the basin and had a weighted line ready. When the spotter gave the signal, we dropped the descent line.

The current at the time of the incident was flowing toward the sea so after dropping the first weight I had another weighted line dropped 10 feet toward sea. My thought was if it was clothes and a knife it would be light and carried a distance by the current before hopefully getting stuck on something on the bottom.

It was 2 am and I was about to put on my helmet when I looked up and saw hundreds of sailors on the ship watching. It sickened everyone that a sailor would rape another sailor onboard our ship at knife point. That woman was our shipmate, and I was sure that the onlookers were willing me to find the evidence that would put the perpetrator away for life in a federal prison.

My helmet had an air supply and communication cable that would connect me with the surface. The other divers would stay on the boat, ready if there was an emergency. They pushed on the helmet and tightened it. I checked the air supply and the communication connection.

"Red diver topside, how do you hear me, Ricky?" Divers were designated by color code, red diver was the lead, green or yellow divers were subordinate to red.

"Loud and clear," I replied.

I chose not to wear fins for this job as they would be cumbersome once I hit the bottom. So, I wore weighted boots instead. Once in the water, I wrapped my legs around the descent line and started my way down. Diving in no visibility pitch dark water was just like diving under ships. I just close my eyes and go to work. As I was descending, I continually said, "Okay, red, okay red, okay red."

Finally, I hit the soup, which felt thicker than the water, so I knew that any second, I would touch down in the mud. I hit the bottom, kneeled, and reported to the surface.

"Topside red diver."

"I hear you. Go ahead, Ricky."

"Job Complete," I responded. "Coming up, red."

I heard shouts over the communications, and someone said: "You better not be joking!"

"Job complete," I repeated. "When I kneeled down, it was under my knee."

Everyone was literally shocked that I'd found that needle in a haystack. Then they asked again if I was certain. "I have an egg-shaped parcel that feels like it could be clothes. I can feel the clothes have been tied in a firm knot and I can feel what I think is a large knife in the middle."

After a pause, I added: "Job complete. Coming up, red. Now pull me up before something down here eats me!" Because I chose to wear boots, I was at the mercy of my tenders on the boat to retrieve me since I couldn't swim.

"Red diver, grab hold of the descent line and prepare to leave the bottom."

"Roger that. Coming up, red."

As I left the bottom, something very sharp cut into my neck, I didn't know if it was a creature taking a bite or a sharp piece of discarded metal. "Hold red, hold red. Lower me back down!" I shouted as the unknown object sliced into my neck.

All the while, I clutched the evidence I'd found as if it were my newborn baby. Once on the bottom again, I reached up to find what was cutting my neck and found an old industrial band saw blade that was rusty and very sharp. I was clearing myself from the hazard when I felt a sharp pain go through my left forearm. I touched the top of my arm and discovered that a sharp piece of jagged metal had gone completely through my wetsuit and forearm and was sticking out the other side.

As a deep-sea diver, you know you are in trouble when you can taste your own blood through your helmet while you breathe. However, we receive countless hours of medical training, so that in the event something happens, you or a teammate can deal with the situation calmly.

Still holding the evidence, I calmly said: "Topside, red diver. I am going to need a medic."

"What's wrong, Ricky?"

"I have a piece of metal that has pierced my forearm. Coming up, red."

I squeezed the evidence as tightly as I could and slowly lifted my arm to release it from the metal object. I needed not only to hold onto the evidence, but to apply direct pressure to both sides of my forearm.

My tenders slowly pulled me up. Once I surfaced, they knew I was in trouble. Several divers jumped in and grabbed me. They all lifted me up and laid me on the deck. As they were lifting my helmet off, the supervisor yelled for me to let go of my arm and the moment I did blood sprayed into the air.

One of my teammates applied pressure to my arm as the dive boat made its way back to the pier. All the while I was clutching the package and would not let go of it. The XO and NCIS team met us on the pier along with an ambulance. Before I handed the evidence over, I said: "We owed this to her."

The injury to my forearm required surgery to ensure no rusty metal was left behind. When I woke up in my hospital room, the XO–who we affectionally called the Hatchet Man– and a few NCIS agents were in my room. I asked if I was in trouble? They said no, just the opposite.

The NCIS agents had some paperwork they needed me to sign regarding the evidence and my custody of it. I told them I never let go of the evidence until it was in their hands. They smiled and one of them said, "Smart boy." The XO congratulated me on a great job and gave me the rest of the week off.

The following week I stepped back onboard *Sierra* with a small bandage on my neck and my forearm in a sling. "Permission to come aboard," I called out to the officer of the deck, and with that my life changed. I was never a popular kid in high school probably because I only went to school three hours a day, since I was on a work-study program, didn't play any sports, and I didn't grow up in that town. So, I always was looked on as an outsider.

On board that day I was far from that high school world, despite my young age. I've never shaken so many hands in my life, every male sailor onboard gave me a nod or a handshake, and every woman gave me a smile or a hug. It was a tragedy that one of our shipmates was raped onboard, but I would be lying if I said I didn't enjoy being popular for the first time in my life. The doctors said for me to take it easy for a couple of weeks and absolutely no diving. So, I just stayed onboard doing administrative work. I was going nuts for two weeks not diving, but finally the doctor cleared me, and I was ready to go to work.

Combatant ships have something called masker belts to protect the vessels from attacks by submarines. The system takes air from the main propulsion gas turbine engines and pressurizes six belts that are attached to the underside of the ship. They have hundreds of little holes in them for the air to escape, creating bubbles that mask the identity of the ship from sonar detection on submarines. The bubbles make it appear that it's simply raining on the surface.

Those hundreds of holes become clogged over time and need to be cleared by divers, who drill into the holes. It was tedious, but an easy job. However, when procedures are altered, even simple underwater tasks can result in disastrous consequences.

The dive was scheduled for the maximum underwater time allowed of 310 minutes. When I arrived to carry out the task, the dive boat was tied alongside the pier on the inside of the ship. I was confused about the boat's position and asked the dive supervisor about it.

He answered that if we tied to the outboard side of the ship, we wouldn't get any lunch from the ship.

I couldn't believe what I was hearing. "So, you expect me to swim all the way under the ship, around the keel and dive on the outboard side just so you guys can get lunch?"

The supervisor laughed and said, "You're a good swimmer, Bettua, and we're all hungry."

I knew I could swim under the ship, but something didn't feel right about this plan. But it was an easy job, I told myself. *Just do it, Rick.*

It only required a few tools, so I grabbed a pin vise, a dozen .125" drill bits, and a magnetic Bear Paws handle to hold onto the ship with. In addition to the tools, I grabbed my own custom harness, and I always wore a red long sleeve shirt over my wetsuit jacket for good luck.

My last act of defiance prior to donning the helmet was to flip the bird to all my teammates for making me swim so far. My air and communication umbilical were three hundred feet long and I would have to use every bit of it to swim to the farthest masker belt on the outboard side. The problem was the current would put additional drag on me, and the longer the umbilical the greater the chance of getting it tangled.

I hopped into the water and did my in-water checks before finally saying, "Topside red diver leaving the surface."

I swam over to the ship, picked a weld on the hull, and followed it down to the keel. From there, I picked up the weld on the outboard side and followed it back up to the surface. From there, I was able to see the masker belts. It's always best to start at the farthest one. That way the tenders could recover the umbilical as I worked my way back to the boat. The Bear Paw handle would hold me in place as I moved along.

Working alone on the hull can be very lonely. While performing a repetitive job underwater, it's easy to begin daydreaming. But I tried to stay focused and drilled each hole out as quickly as I could. I was about ten feet from the keel, but I needed slack in the umbilical to go back up to start the next belt. I called out to topside and asked them to slack red, but nothing happened.

I yelled out for them to stop eating and give me some slack. Finally, the dive supervisor's voice came through, and he told me to follow my umbilical down to the keel to see if it was fouled. I started to pull myself down and it wasn't long before I touched the muddy bottom. The high tide that day was unusually high, which meant the low tide would be lower than normal. I immediately called up to the dive supervisor and told him we had a problem.

"What is it, Rick?"

I told him that the ship had settled down on my umbilical and I couldn't get back to the inboard side. What made the matter worse was the tide was still going out and, as it did, it was pushing my umbilical deeper and deeper in the mud which also brought me closer and closer to the keel.

I'm pretty sure everyone's lunch went flying as they all jumped up to devise a plan. The problem was the dive boat couldn't move while I was underwater, and the standby diver couldn't get to me because he didn't have enough umbilical to swim around the ship.

As the ship continued to settle, I had less and less umbilical and was now standing on the bottom with very little slack. I called up and said, "Topside red diver. It's getting tight down here. I am going to ditch."

Those words are something a diving supervisor never wants to hear, and he yelled for me not to do it. He was concerned I wouldn't make it. Ditching a helmet and unclipping your lifeline would take too long.

But what choice did I have? I was sitting on my butt and the ship was pressing down on me. I called up to the supervisor. "You better do something quick before I get buried alive."

The easy task had turned into a deadly endeavor. I'd already released my umbilical and was at the point where I was ready to pull off my helmet. I would do it as quickly as I could, then blow and go all the way to the surface. I wouldn't be able to hold my breath as I went up, because my lungs would expand, causing an air embolism. So, I would need to blow out.

My hand was on the helmet's spider, and I was about to ditch when I heard the noise of divers coming down on the outboard side. One diver squeezed under the ship with me while the other diver tended him from the bilge keel. He had a lightweight mask for me which was easier to get on and off. On the count of three, we pulled my helmet off, and he slapped the mask on my face. The mask was attached to an umbilical, so I had air as we headed to the surface. To my amazement, when I reached the surface, I saw the USS *Cable*'s dive boat in front of me. The *Cable* is a submarine tender that was working several piers down. They'd dropped everything to come to my rescue.

I crawled up onto the dive platform of the dive boat and pulled off my mask. In front of me was their master diver, who had a huge smile on his face. "Son, you look like a mud-rat." He was right. I was covered in mud. "What are you doing diving the outboard side of the ship with your dive boat on the inside?"

"Those assholes wanted lunch, so they had me swim under the ship," I explained.

He looked seriously at me. "At any time did you feel something was wrong with what you were doing?"

"Yes, but I didn't want to say anything."

"Son, if it don't feel right, it ain't right. You remember that."

He asked me my name, and when I told him, Petty Officer Second Class Rick Bettua, one of his chiefs nodded, and said that I was the one. The master chief laughed and said, "Now this makes sense, since you're the one who found the evidence on that rapist a few weeks ago."

He shook my hand and said, "Good job, Ricky."

CHAPTER 6

BAD COMMS

The ship was underway for the remote island of Diego Garcia in the Indian Ocean to relieve the current tender that was on station. Diego Garcia is in the British Indian Ocean Territory and is approximately a thousand miles east of Africa and a thousand miles South of India. The U.S. military leases the island and operates an Air Force base as well as a Navy refueling depot. It is a beautiful tropical atoll near the equator with safe anchorage inside its massive lagoon. I had never heard of the island, so I went up to see the Quartermasters to look at a chart. The moment I saw the chart I knew the waters around the island would be loaded with fish.

As we sailed through the Mediterranean, we stopped in several key countries for port visits. All of them were equally spectacular, many I had visited the year before while aboard the *Stump*. Finally, we arrived at the entrance to the Suez Canal and waited our turn to pass through. After seeing how narrow the canal was, I could not believe we were going to squeeze through. But just then a super tanker larger than us passed through, so I guessed it was going to be fine. The brief voyage through the canal is like a history lesson. You can see discarded military vehicles and the yellow fleet, which consists of stranded vessels from eight different countries. The fifteen ships were trapped there when the canal was shut during a war between Egypt and Israel. It's called the yellow fleet because during the eight years of entrapment, sand has caused them to turn yellow.

Diego Garcia is shaped like a foot and the entrance to the lagoon is surrounded by beautiful coral reefs. The inside of the lagoon is a perfect anchorage that can accommodate many surface ships and submarines. It has a constant water depth inside the lagoon of 115 to 140 feet while outside of the atoll, the depth drops quickly to thousands of feet.

Our job was to provide diving services to both surface ships and submarines, so our first order of business was to use the ship's crane to get our dive boat into the water. The *Sierra* had two large booms on each side of the ship that were used to moor small boats. One of them was designated for us and it wasn't long before we were ready to go to work.

Every day we would get dive jobs assigned to us in order of priority from the ship's repair officer. We would grab our equipment and head out on the dive boat. It was nice working away from the ship, because it provided a bit of freedom and the crews from the other ships treated us well, and always fed us better than what we got on the *Sierra*.

On the weekends, if we weren't working, we were allowed to use the dive boat to explore the island and even spearfish. I could hardly believe what I saw the first time I slipped into the crystal-clear waters. It was like being home in South Florida again, but with a lot more fish and all the fish were big. I primarily targeted coral trout as they were like what I was shooting at home and the average fish size was about twenty to forty pounds per fish.

Although my teammates didn't spearfish, they all wanted to help, and we came up with a system that was a bit like an assembly line. I would make the shot and grab the fish, then pass it to the other divers, and they would attempt to get it in the boat. Seems simple, but it was hilarious as they knew nothing about fish, and many fish escaped. The first day we went back to the ship, we all walked onboard toting a nice fish, showing off our prowess underwater. Half of the fish went to the ship's main cooks and the other half went to the chiefs' mess cooks.

One day the repair officer came up to the dive locker to let us know a frigate was on its way to the harbor with a vibration in its running gear, and we needed to check it out quickly. Frigates are smaller in design than destroyers and have a single shaft propeller system while the destroyers have twin shafts.

We were in the dive boat waiting on the ship to anchor. Once aboard, I asked what the problem was and then carried out a safety check, known as tagging the ship. Ships and submarines have many items that could hurt and possibly kill a diver underwater. Tagging the ship involves locating the controls for those devices and hanging a red tag on them that says, "Do not operate. Divers in the water." The tags must be signed by both the engineering officer and the command duty officer.

The ship's engineer told me they were hearing an unusual noise coming from just forward of the propeller. "Roger that, sir. We'll check it out," I replied.

My good friend, Bib, and I were sort of the A-team onboard where diving was concerned, and we were chosen to do the job. After we slipped into the water and did our normal in-water checks, we both raced down to the propeller, and we could not believe our eyes. Just forward of the propeller is a V-shaped strut that supports the weight of the shaft and propeller; stuck in that V between the strut and the bottom of the ship, was a massive dead ocean sunfish. We tried to move it, but it was huge and probably weighed more than a ton.

We headed up to the surface to discuss our next step. The ship's captain and engineer were hanging over the main deck of the ship when we removed our helmets and asked straight away what the problem was. We explained what we found, and the captain said, "A fish, you say?"

"A very big fish." It was late in the afternoon, and we decided to stop diving so we could come up with a plan to remove it.

One of the best things about being a Navy diver is the Navy always ensured we were well equipped for any contingency. Among the equipment we'd taken from our base in South Carolina was a portable hydraulic tool package that could operate a variety of underwater tools including drills, impact wrenches, jaws of life, and even an underwater chainsaw.

We had a meeting with the repair officer and when we laid out our plan for getting the sunfish clear of the ship's strut, he asked what support we needed. There were seven hundred shipmates aboard and all were willing to help in any way that they could. I replied that we needed three engineers who could operate a diesel-powered hydraulic tool. The dive team only had enough personnel to man our dive stations.

If we divers were apprehensive about anything, it was the sharks in the lagoon. Every night we saw dozens cruising around our ship under the lights and we didn't know how they would react once we started cutting up a ton of sushi. For this job we used two divers in hardhats with communications, and I would dive scuba to ensure the safety of the other divers. I was used to diving around sharks and battling them for runaway fish when I was younger. But for this dive I would remain alert for any hungry intruders and carry a six-foot-long 12-gauge bang stick that could kill even the biggest shark and.

I got in first to ensure the area was safe. The day before, while doing the inspection of the propeller, we noticed only three or four sharks, but now that number had increased to more than thirty. I returned to the dive boat and told the others what I had seen.

The diving officer wanted to call off the dive, but I assured her I could provide a safety net, and no one would get hurt. I heard someone say, "How do you plan on doing that?"

I grabbed six shotgun shells and said I'm going to kill the biggest one right now and with that I slid into the water and picked out a very solid ten-foot whaler. Most sharks in the Pacific and Indian Oceans are in the whaler family (tiger, bull, and grey reef). The big whaler was not scared of me and as I got close to it the other sharks were now getting closer to me.

The moment that 12-gauge hit its head the noise was deafening. It just rolled over and died then slowly sank to the bottom of the lagoon with a trail of blood following it. After that, the other sharks scattered. The job itself was very easy and uneventful, the divers only needed to make a few cuts with the chainsaw to get the giant sunfish dislodged, all the while I sat atop of the propeller as security, ensuring no sharks returned.

While onboard *Sierra*, each division got an allowance of beer each quarter and could drink that beer during a scheduled division party. We chose a beautiful Saturday to have our division party and used the dive boat to go spearfishing for a few hours, then we transported everyone in our division to a secluded beach on the far side of the lagoon.

As the six of us divers walked down the gangway, we each had a case of beer on our shoulder, and we also had six girls that we'd invited along from the ship. Half-way down to the boat, I heard the Hatchet Man, our executive officer, say, "Petty Officer Bettua, may I have a word, please?"

As I walked back up to the main deck, I thought he was either going to say put the beer back, or the girls can't go. To my surprise, he simply asked me if I could bring back a couple of nice fish for the officer's mess. I smiled and said, "I'll take care of that right now, sir, before we start our division party."

Everyone onboard was afraid of the XO. After all, there was a reason for his nickname. Sure, he was firm, but that was his job as an executive officer, and he was also fair. For some reason, he liked the divers, and always looked after us.

We were allowed to exercise as much as we liked and one day we were working out during a thunderstorm on the ship's fantail, which was about thirty feet above the water. It was pouring hard when we saw something odd. The captain's gig (boat) had broken free of the boom securing it, and was floating past us, which seemed very surreal. As we all gazed out at the boat in the rough sea, the XO showed up and screamed, "What do I pay you for?" Then he pointed at the captain's gig and said, "Fetch!"

All six of us dove off the ship together and it took us over an hour of hard swimming to catch up and board the drifting vessel. We drove the captain's boat back, tied it up, and then boarded the ship to find the XO waiting for us. He smiled and simply said, "Good job, boys." It wasn't much, but we appreciated any recognition for a task well done.

Our cruise was extended several times and with each extension tempers onboard became shorter and shorter. While crossing the Atlantic, it seemed like each day fights were breaking out in the mess hall, and the XO reached out for us to help. He said that he noticed the six of us always did everything together and then he asked if we could act as a team of bouncers to get the hot heads under control. It didn't take long before everyone got the message. There might have been a few sailors who might take on two of us, but not all six.

Our message was loud and clear. It was okay to disagree but keep your hands to yourself. The moment any sailors raised their voices in the chow hall, we would all get up without hesitation and go sit next to them. The fact that we were now involved seemed to calm the crew down. The ship returned to Charleston, South Carolina in the summer of 1982 for a well-deserved stand-down period. But the divers would not see one day of it. The largest auxiliary ship stationed in Charleston was pulling in with a damaged propeller.

The very next morning Bib and I were on the inspection team and even with poor visibility it didn't take long to find out the ship had a propeller blade that was folded over. This propeller to date was the largest I had ever seen at close to twenty feet in diameter and weighing nearly forty tons. To make matters worse, during our inspection we noticed the hull had no pad eyes welded above the propeller.

If divers were to change this propeller while the ship was waterborne, it would require the use of a balance beam. This would complicate things immensely as a balance beam is nothing more than a huge steel teeter totter, which in this case would hold a forty-ton propeller on one end and a forty-ton weight on the other. A crane would lower the balance beam and that would allow us to reach under the ship far enough to get the old propeller off the shaft, and the new one on. But it wouldn't be easy. When Bib and I resurfaced, we gave each other a look that said we hoped the ship would go into dry dock to be repaired.

While we never back down from any job, we were not jumping at the opportunity to change this propeller underwater, either. We had only eight divers in our dive locker, and even if we brought personnel in to help with the topside rigging and to operate the engineering equipment, we would still be stretched thin.

A meeting took place between the repair officer and other officers on board, and they made the decision to task the *Sierra* dive locker with the job of removing and replacing the auxiliary ship's propeller. The Navy maintains the necessary equipment to conduct propeller changes at storage depots around the world and within a short period of time everything we needed showed up. The hydraulic system we would use to pressurize the propeller and break it free is called a pilgrim nut. The system is comprised of relatively few parts: the pilgrim nut, studs, and a strongback girder. The pilgrim nut itself would thread onto the shaft and then we could expand it with a hydraulic pump, which would provide enough rearward force to pop the propeller free. As a team, we studied the procedure repeatedly to ensure everyone was clear on their positions and the tasks assigned.

Once the new propeller showed up, we were ready to get to work. Bib and I worked flawlessly together as a dive team and spoke very little because we knew each other so well. Besides, back in those days the communication system was more of a problem than it was worth. Although propeller changes are a major undertaking underwater, the procedure for small or large propellers is the exact same.

The first thing to do was to rotate the shaft so the lifting pad eye on the propeller was in the 12 o'clock position. Then remove the plug and thread in the pad eye. Then the next task was to remove the massive bronze dunce cap. The dunce cap covers the boss nut to streamline the running gear causing fewer bubbles and making the system more efficient and silent. It is a massive thing weighing more than a ton and a crane would be needed to lift it to the surface. After it was unbolted, we headed to the surface to discuss the crane lift.

We were using a Navy YD Floating Crane, a massive crane built atop of an eighty-foot barge capable of lifting one hundred and fifty tons. As Bib and I were sitting on the dive platform, Bib's hardhat was removed, and he went to speak to the crane operator. I just sat on the platform with my legs dangling in the water. When you get a break between dives, it's nice just to zone out and not think, giving your brain a break because underwater you need to constantly focus.

While I sat there watching the current ebbing, I saw a large log coming toward me and just at that moment I was yanked off the swim platform up to the deck of the boat in one swift movement. Bib grabbed me and pointed at the log which actually was a twelve-foot alligator. We called South Carolina Fish and Game, were told they would capture and then relocate the beast.

The alligator remained in the area where we would be diving, but no one was going into the water while it was still prowling about. Once the game and fish officer arrived, we pointed at the gator, and he took out what we thought was a tranquilizer gun. But when it went off, we were startled. It was a 30.06, and the beast just rolled over. The officer then asked if I would tie a line to it.

I had two questions: What happed to the relocation program, and are you sure it's dead? He replied that it was too big to relocate, and added, "Yes, son. Its dead."

Although using the balance beam complicated the job, the rest of the propeller removal went smoothly. The following day we arrived to find the crane crew and engineers busy setting up the massive balance beam with the shiny new propellor on one end and a massive concrete weight on the other. To add to the already expansive rigging involved, a chain fall was added to the propeller side of the beam. This would allow us divers to fine tune and make minor adjustments in order to slide the propeller onto the shaft.

Getting the propeller onto the tapered shaft without getting it cocked or jammed requires that the shaft is moved to the center of the propeller's hub. The three feet of visibility would make this process more difficult, but Bib and I would slow everything down and check and recheck each other to ensure the propeller would go on perfectly. If a propeller gets jammed and you are using a balance beam, it is difficult to apply the correct direction of force to unjam it.

The communication system between surface and divers continued to function inadequately, and even after alterations were made, it was fair at best. Despite that, we decided to give it a try. The diving supervisor said he only wanted me to communicate with the crane operator. That way the operator wouldn't get confused with two other voices and a second conversation.

Once in the water, Bib and I swam over to the rigging monstrosity. The balance beam with eighty tons attached to it slowly descended. I would remain at the hub of the propeller as it came down, while Bib, who was at the other end of the beam, would keep things aligned ninety degrees to the shaft. The visibility was a bit better, maybe six feet, and I could see Bib silhouetted with the sun behind him.

As the crane continued to lower the beam, I looked past the hub and started seeing the shaft. When it was close, I called out to the crane operator, "Hold that."

Everything was aligned to the right and left, but we needed to come down just slightly. I asked to come up and speak to the crane operator. I swam up and the operator was waiting for me. I explained to him that when I say come down, I wanted him to start and stop immediately. I held my fingers up to show him the slightest amount. I also said that would be the command, "Start-stop." He nodded in agreement and said he understood.

I swam back down to the shaft and now Bib was on the port side, and I was on the starboard side of the shaft. We both were holding onto the shaft and looking aft at the propeller hub when I said, "Start-stop." The propeller came slightly down, stopped, then rocked forward toward us. It was sliding onto the tapered shaft and I said, "Hold that!" I wanted to let everything settle down.

For whatever reason, the crane operator thought I said, "Coming down," and the balance beam started to lower the forty-ton weight while the propeller was only partially on the shaft. Like a great big teeter-totter, it wobbled, and the propeller slid off the shaft and was gone. The first thing I saw was the massive blade narrowly missing my face, then impacting the shaft with enough force to cut a car in half. I could see it was going to slice down on the port side where Bib was stationed.

I reached over the shaft, grabbed Bib by the harness, and pulled him up and over the shaft before the propeller could smash down the side he was on. During the ordeal, his umbilical and air supply had been crushed and I needed to clear it. Once everything stopped moving, we returned to the surface. We were both so rattled by the near-death experience that we halted the operation for the day.

CHAPTER 7

SECURITY ALERT

Weeks later, I was in the dive locker doing some administrative work logging all our dives with the Naval Safety Center. An older man in civilian clothes sporting a massive mustache and a wad of chewing tobacco just walked in and spit in the waste can. I jumped up and said, "Are you fucking kidding me?"

He stared at me and said, "Boy, taking this shit-can out to the pier is going to be good liberty for you. I'm your new senior chief."

In short order, the senior chief recognized I was doing more than what I was qualified to handle as a second-class diver. "Let me see if I got this right," he said. "You are the leading diver and you are qualified as a diving supervisor, but you're a second-class diver?"

"That's right, Senior Chief."

"Why did you decide to become a diving supervisor?"

"No one else wanted to do it."

"Well, young man, if you are good enough to qualify as a dive supervisor, you should be a first-class diver and from what I can see one day you will become a master diver."

When I said that I thought I needed to be a second-class diver for at least three years, he replied, "No, you're heading to first-class dive school right now."

First-class dive school was in Panama City, Florida and it was just as much fun and as challenging as second-class school, but a lot more homework. My classmates came from a variety of duty stations and all of them had a vast amount of experience. I would form a friendship with some of them that would last for decades. Like a big family, we trained hard together, we studied together, and we partied together.

I had never seen so many pretty girls in my life as I saw on Panama City Beach during spring break, which was out of control. Thousands upon thousands of country girls had descended upon the beach, which lived up to its nickname as the Redneck Riviera.

In fact, more of my classmates were getting dropped from training for alcohol related incidents than anything else. Although I had fun, I never drank too much. Upon graduation, I was the honor man and I got first pick of orders anywhere. When I told the master chief detailer I wanted to go somewhere and dive as much as possible he just laughed and said, "Okay, young man, be careful what you asked for."

Groton Submarine Base in Connecticut is the world's largest submarine base and at that time over thirty divers were assigned to manage its massive fleet. Reporting for duty in the middle of winter in New England was challenging. Snow and ice covered the ground, and the Thames River was frozen over.

I went inside to report for duty, and during my check, the master diver (Ray) seemed disappointed. So, I asked if everything was okay. He replied that I wasn't what he had asked for. He needed a leading petty officer to run the YDT-2 boat and crew. "You are too young and only a second-class petty officer."

With that, he called the master chief/master diver detailer at the Pentagon, and they had a loud conversation. I heard the detailer say, "I know he's young, but he's the best of the best."

The master diver argued that I was too young, and the detailer fired back, "Give him a chance, Ray."

With that, the phone went dead, and I thought, *What a way to start out.*

The master diver told me to follow him and he walked me out to introduce me to my crew. En route, he explained the problem was that I was only a second-class petty officer, and others in my crew were senior in rank as well as older. He said they wouldn't appreciate me telling them what to do. "You better become a first-class petty officer as soon as you can."

I'd received the same message from my last master diver, but that was about becoming a first-class diver. Now that I was one, I was being told I also needed to quickly become a first-class petty officer. When I was introduced to everyone, I could tell a few faces in the crew were not happy, but so be it. My new crew then grabbed me and tossed me into the icy water and that was my initiation.

The master diver and I had what I would call a love-hate relationship. He would ride me to do more and more dive jobs, and when I got those done, I wouldn't so much as get a smile from him. Then he would hand me a list of half a dozen more. One day he came out to all us divers holding a computer printout. He said, "There is a right way, and there is a wrong way, then there is Bettua's way of doing things." He looked at me and said, "How can you be doing this many jobs?" My answer was that I had a really good crew, and the room erupted in laughter.

I think that was the day the master diver finally cracked his first smile at me. I dove as much as I could and instead of taking a break between dives, I would supervise the next dive. At least the divers on my boat knew I could dive, and I wasn't afraid to show them. With sometimes two or three dive crews working around the clock, my crew always wanted the night shift, and that was fine with me. Working at night got us away from the brass. We knew how to dive and could get more done at night with no one bothering us.

I adopted a policy that on every dive, red diver would be an experienced senior diver, and green diver would be an inexperienced kid. This insured they got trained the right way from the beginning. We had some exceptional divers in my boat, and one would later become a master diver, as would I, and we would stay friends for another twenty years.

There was a bit of rivalry between the Navy divers and the Marines who provided security for the base. Much like us, they were all athletic and every time the base had any sort of sporting competition our master chief and their sergeant major would challenge each other to see who had the best team. One year there was to be a smoker's match, which is boxing. It involved three rounds, three minutes each, nine minutes of all-out slug fests in different weight classes.

Almost immediately after asking, the master diver had five divers willing to give it a go. I was not only staying out of it, but I also wanted nothing to do with it. After the divers weighed in, they were one weight class short, 155 pounds. The master diver looked around the room and said, Bettua, come here. I knew what was coming next and when he asked me if I would participate, I told him I knew nothing about boxing. That was okay, he said, and told me I would do fine.

Once dressed, I scanned the Marines to find a competitor my size but couldn't find anyone. When they called my weight class, I entered the ring, my gloves and headgear on tight, and waited for my opponent. He was a head taller than me, and the announcer said he was from Corpus Christi, Texas and had appeared in thirty-two fights.

Round one went well, and we were about even. I noticed right away that he couldn't hit that hard if I stayed in close. But if I gave him room, his punches would sting. At the end of Round two, I hit him with a combination, and he stumbled back. The referee gave him a standing eight-count, which put us into round three. When the bell rang, the marine came out and hit me on top of my head forcing my headgear down over my eyes and the ref held his hands up to fix my headgear. As he did so, the Marine hit me squarely under my left eye.

The punch cut open my face and blood splattered about the ring. The Marine was disqualified, and I went to the emergency room to get stitched up. The next morning the left side of my face was black and blue, and I had six stitches in my face. At our morning meeting, other divers were giggling. The master diver walked up to me and told everyone that I looked the way I did because he asked me to compete. Then he told me to take the rest of the week off, that I deserved it.

One day the sergeant major came down and had a meeting with the master diver regarding security at the lower base, specifically protecting the submarines. His Marines needed to be trained and he wanted us to provide a real-world exercise via a training event. The master diver wanted insurance that none of his divers would get hurt. After all, the Marines would not know it was staged and would be responding to the threat with loaded weapons. The sergeant major assured him not only would he be on station, but several other senior Marines would be as well, to ensure things didn't go wrong. The base security officer, the commanding officer, and the admiral were all informed about the security test. However, very few Marines knew it was only a test and that was considered key, because they didn't want the security team to know anything.

The master diver brought me in and briefed me on the task, which was more complicated than most knew, and would require a combined effort of multiple organizations. He chose a submarine that was in a "cold plant" status, which meant the submarine's nuclear reactor was shut down and the ship was in a refurbishment period. It also meant the sub was already completely "Tagged Out" for diving operations. The tag out program is no joke on a submarine because there are so many different underwater hazards both mechanical and electrical that can kill a diver.

We needed port control to play its part by shutting down all boat traffic on the Thames River and they would also need to task the tug department to break up the ice on the river just prior to our mission. The day before the security test, I personally went to every organization involved to ensure they knew what their position was and answer any questions they might have. I chose to wait until the last minute to pick my team and even then, I didn't tell them about the job until the morning of the event.

When it comes to diving, even the best laid plans can fall apart in a fraction of a second, and this exercise unfortunately would be proof of that. I told my team they had one hour to get ready and that the four of us would be diving scuba from the far side of the river to our intended target for an assault. The three divers who would join me were very excited since this was something out of the norm. I explained to them the sub was tagged out and we would be exiting the water and boarding at the turtle back. That's the rear of the submarine and the closest point to the waterline, making it the easiest place for us to board the sub.

We would all be wearing twin tanks and would be tethered together. The other first-class diver and I would also wear compasses. The distance from the far side of the river to our intended target was less than a thousand yards. I told my team we would leave the surface and stay ten feet off the bottom while crossing the river.

The Thames was dark, clear water, and we would have no problem seeing the bottom from ten feet. This was important because the river itself provided two pieces of information that would assist us in swimming in a straight line. The river bottom is muddy and the ripples in the mud are always at a 90-degree angle to the flow of the river. Also, the tide was coming in so the current would be coming from our right. With those two bits of data and a compass, I was confident we could swim straight and undetected.

We all were dressed out sitting in the Boston Whaler, which was covered with snow, as we watched the tugs breaking up the ice. Finally, it was done and the massive sheet of ice that stretched from our side of the river to the opposite side had been broken up into small pieces. We were getting cold just sitting there as the boat slowly moved toward our entry point. When we reached it, we slid into the icy water, and it was a relief since the water was warmer than the air temperature and there was no wind chill factor.

We did our in-water checks, gave each other okays, then left the surface. The water was clear and the ripples on the mud were pronounced and easy to see. After about fifteen minutes, I wanted to take a sneak peek to ensure we were on target, so I gave hand signals for all of us to come up to ten feet below the surface. I unhooked from my partner and went up for a quick one-second look. We were in the perfect location and should hit our intended target in another fifteen minutes. I clipped back in, gave the boys an okay and we continued.

Focusing on a compass and the bottom can get monotonous, but right on cue after fifteen minutes of swimming I looked up to see our target's massive propeller. Once we approached the submarine, I felt a sigh of relief and we staged ourselves on the stern plane—a flat extension like wings on either side of a sub—where we unhooked from one another, then swam up to the turtle back. To my amazement it was solid ice, and we couldn't break through to board the sub.

We then swam forward and tried to get through the ice in several places, but it was too thick. We were at the sonar dome on the forward end of the submarine when one of my divers showed me that he was getting low on air. Suddenly, it wasn't a simple security alert training mission any longer, but a potential catastrophe, if I didn't quickly come up with a new plan.

I had no choice but to get my team out of the water quickly and the only option was risky and very dangerous. I motioned for all of them to follow me and we returned to our intended target's nuclear reactor, which was midship on the submarine. Several submarines were lined up and moored on a row of piers. The sub on the next pier was going to sea later that day, and I knew she would have her reactor turned on. I took a bearing, then we swam slowly under the ice to the other submarine. The crew of that sub had no idea that we were coming, and the sub wasn't tagged out for diving operations.

I kept everyone behind me as I wanted to ensure we didn't get near a main seawater pump which could kill us. I saw the submarine directly in front of me and it was a perfect hit. We were at the ship's reactor where the water was like slush from the heat coming off the ship. We popped to the surface with our hands above our heads and were greeted by several M-16s pointed at us.

We heard the sirens on the base and an amplified voice saying: "Security alert! Security alert!" as the base was being shut down. The armed crew members on the sub's main deck screamed at us to not move. I looked over at our intended target on the other pier and saw the master diver and several senior officers all abandoning that pier and running to get to this one. I told my team not to move.

The weapons pointing at us were loaded and the crew pointing them at us were very nervous. The Marine Corps Security Alert Team arrived and quickly took charge of the scene, and they were even more hyped up than the crew of the submarine. They shouted at us not to move and keep our hands on our heads.

I saw the master diver and admiral boarding the submarine and they didn't look happy. The senior member of the security team motioned for us to come up one at a time. Our tanks were removed, and we were handcuffed and searched. I was last to climb the ladder and I got to the deck just as the master diver and admiral arrived. A couple of over-zealous Marines kicked my legs out from under me with my tanks still on my back and slammed me to the deck. My master diver charged one of the Marines and had to be restrained from assaulting him.

The admiral shouted, "End of drill!" That's when everyone knew it was staged. I was helped up to my feet by my teammates and my mouth was cut and bleeding. The admiral and master diver asked what happened, why we had come to a submarine that was lit off. Was it a mistake, did we get we lost? I explained what happened and why I decided we needed to swim to the adjacent submarine. It was a gamble, but the only thing I could think of at the time. We were trapped under the ice and two of the divers were low on air. The master diver said, "Smart boy, Ricky," and the admiral agreed the decision I made prevented others in my team from getting hurt or possibly killed.

In the aftermath, the master diver remained angered about how the Marines manhandled us, and he didn't hold back telling the sergeant major what he thought about the incident. We knew the Marines had come out on top and we divers were waiting for the right time to retaliate. The Marines had a mascot at their barracks, a beautiful white English bulldog. One day the dog was kidnapped, and the kidnappers shaved the dog's ass and painted one cheek blue and the other gold, which are the official Navy colors.

CHAPTER 8

TOUGH LOVE

It was a beautiful summer day in Connecticut in 1985 when the master diver called Scott and me into his office to put us on a new project. Although Scott and I were friends, we were also competitors, and we didn't normally work together. I oversaw the YDT-2 Dive Boat and Scott was in charge of the YDT-1 Dive Boat.

In fact, I could only think of one time we worked together and that was on a difficult job to change a propeller that took us only sixteen hours to accomplish over two days right before Christmas. The master diver, who wanted to be home for the holiday, came down to supervise, sending six divers at a time to work on replacing the prop of a 688-class submarine.

Now our new task sounded like a lot more fun. We were going to represent Navy divers at the Connecticut State Fair. The Connecticut State Troopers had a viewing tank on a trailer that we could use for a display. However, we would be required to clean the tank and paint it and the trailer.

Scott and I went over with a one-ton truck and picked up the viewing tank from the troopers. It was much larger than both of us envisioned, about ten-foot square with a massive viewing window in the front. The tank itself was rusting and looked in overall poor condition, and the trailer was on its last leg, cracked in a few places. Scott was a hull technician, which was a welder, and he could fix that. But the trailer and tank would need to be chipped, ground down, then primed and painted in order to look good enough for us to use it in a show.

I remember when we got back to the diving locker the master

chief came out for a look and said three words, "Get to work." With both boat crews on-hand, we had plenty of manpower. So, it wasn't long before the viewing tank was back in pristine condition with a coat of blue and gold paint, the Navy's colors. We were going to the fair!

The plan was simple. The master chief wanted at least four different diving rigs at the fair. Mark V was the classic copper and brass helmet, Mk-12 was the Navy's newest replacement for the old heavy helmet. We also had the AGA, the rig we used day in and day out when diving on submarines. It's a lightweight mask that was easy to take on and off. Finally, we included scuba gear for our display.

Scott and I met with the master diver to discuss the display and, to our amazement, he wanted not only a Navy diver in the tank waving to everybody walking by, but also to offer civilians a chance to get in the tank with the diver! We choose ten young divers who would represent us well at the fair, and either Scott or I would supervise the dives. Even 10 feet of water can cause a life-threatening air embolism should an inexperienced person hold their breath coming up and the master diver wanted to ensure no one was hurt.

The day finally arrived for the fair to begin and our Navy diver display absolutely trumped every other display at the fair ground. The tank was filled with over 2500 gallons of water and everyone wanted to get in and cool off. The master diver sat in the background next to a keg of beer with a massive smile on his face. He was proud for several reasons, but I think the biggest one was the Marines had their display right next to us and it was garbage. All day long people were lining up to have a try at either diving Mk-V or Mk-12 and as the day went on, the participants were getting younger and younger.

One headstrong little girl came up to me and asked if she could try. Her parents were standing there and I asked how old she was and they said nine. Of course, she was way too small to fit in a suit so whatever we did with her would require some thought. I pointed at the master diver and told her to ask that scary man if she could go in the tank.

She walked right up to him and said, "I hear you are the

only person standing in my way of giving that a try."

The master diver cocked his head, looked at Scott and me, then stood up, took the girl's hand and walked over to us. "Ricky and Scott, you both get dressed out. I'll supervise this."

When we were ready, we both sat at the top of the tank with AGA masks on holding a Mk-V helmet for our new little diver. The master diver said for us to hold the helmet on her and support her under her arms. We got her in the tank and she was fearless. With Scott on one side and me on the other, we walked her down the ladder in front of a crowd of onlookers. At the bottom, she waved to her parents. Little did she know at the time the two guys supporting her would become the next generation of the Navy master divers.

It was good to see the master diver in a different light during the state fair. He was always tough for me to read and even more difficult to work for, and he never accepted second best at anything. But for all the difficulties he caused us, he protected us like a mother bear protecting her cubs. No one and I mean no one on that base was allowed to challenge us without feeling his wrath. If a chief or officer on a submarine raised their voice to us or wanted us to do something not planned, our master diver put them in their place.

By now, I was a first-class petty officer and with that ranking came more responsibilities, and one day the master diver announced I needed to grab a six-man scuba team and head to Nova Scotia as quickly as I could pack. I asked what the job was and he said it was a security swim on a pier and a Trident missile submarine.

I replied to the master diver, "That's a long way."

He told us to drive to Portland, Maine and the next morning take a ferry to Nova Scotia. "Roger that, Master Chief," I said and headed out.

We were all looking forward to getting off the base for a while, and it was an easy four-hour drive to Portland where we checked into a nice hotel. The receptionist smiled and told us that we were in luck that there was a great band playing tonight in the bar and the place would be packed with girls. She told us to come down at 9 pm and she'd give us passes to get in and get a free drink. Portland didn't disappoint us and we did our very best to show them why sailors have more fun, as the saying goes.

The next morning came early, though, as we needed to be at the ferry by 0600. But to our surprise and disappointment, when we arrived at the ferry station, we found a sign at the entrance that read, "Ferry Closed until Spring."

I called the master diver with the news and his response was that we better get driving because we had less than twenty hours before "show time"—the arrival of the submarine at the port. We pulled out a map and discovered we had a twelve-hour drive ahead of us to Halifax. Due to a few of Canada's Royal Mounted Police officers, it took us fourteen hours to get there, and we were almost arrested for being in possession of a standard Navy dive knife.

We reached the Naval Air Station in Halifax just a few hours before the submarine arrived. We went straight to work, checking out the pier where the Trident would tie up. The water was clear and no bombs were visible. It was an easy job and uneventful. The sub pulled in like clockwork and after tagging her out, we dove again and examined the sub's hull.

Our mission was to stay on station in Nova Scotia until the Trident was ready to go back to sea and then perform another check of the massive submarine and pier for bombs. We showed up to do our final swim on the sub, but the water under the pier was missing. Nova Scotia is subject to massive tides and the tide was unusually low. The water had receded more than thirty feet where the submarine was located.

The Canadian divers put a ladder out for us, but I wasn't game to try and go down a flexible rope ladder with a set of twin tanks on my back. As the smallest member in the team, I made the best decision for me, which would be to jump the three stories with the twin tanks on.

The Canadians were amazed I would even try to jump that distance and they gathered around to watch. I stood up, cinched everything down tight, gave an okay to the diving supervisor, and without hesitation stepped off the pier. Sure, I was scared and it hurt like hell on impact, but I was not about to give any of them the satisfaction of laughing. In fact, the reaction was just the opposite. The Canadians were astonished, even envious. The other divers on the team went down the rope ladder and that was an absolute nightmare trying to control themselves on nothing more than a rope swing. After everything was cleared, the submarine left port and we all headed back to Connecticut and the base in Groton.

It was striper season in the Northeast. Striper are a beautiful powerful fish that can grow up to eighty pounds, and I had an idea they were at the base lurking under the piers. I brought my speargun in to work one day and my idea was to have a look under the pier at lunch time. While everyone was inside the dive locker eating lunch and watching Divorce Court on television, I slipped into the water behind the YDT-2 boat next to the pier.

I went under it and started to calm down as my eyes adjusted to the darkness. The water under the pier was dark, but very clear. On my very first drop, while lying on the bottom, I heard the telltale boom of a big stripers tail. I returned to the surface for air and tried to stay calm. I knew big fish were near.

Sliding back to the bottom thirty feet down, I got into position. I could feel my heart pumping and I willed it to slow down. The fish knew I was there. They could hear me and came in to look. I spotted the big striper, and the moment I had a clear shot, I took it and the fish was dispatched in an instant.

I hit the surface under the pier holding my prize, which was close to thirty-five pounds, and I slowly swam back to the boat and dive platform. I was sitting on the dive platform admiring my prize when I heard the master diver shouting my name. I tried to jump up and hide my fish, but he was already standing above me.

"Where did you get that?" he asked.

"Under the pier."

"Well, you better go back and get one for you, because that one belongs to me."

"Roger that, Master Chief."

The master diver and I had that sort of arrangement, ever since I went to work for him. Not many Navy divers or commercial divers, I would guess, cared to pursue diving as a hobby in their spare time. But for me, and a few others at the command, we couldn't get enough. We would dive all week and ask the master diver if we could go bugging (our term for catching lobsters) on the weekend.

Every time I asked the master diver if I could use the boat to dive on the weekend, he would say two things. First, he would ask: "How many divers you got?" Then he would say, "Okay, but don't forget about me."

So, after our dive we would all divvy up our bounty and the master diver always got a take. For me, it was never about how many lobsters I could bring home. It was all about fun and I loved diving for them because it was similar to spearfishing. Diving for Maine lobster was like an easter egg hunt. It was just you and a light. After getting to the bottom, you would move up and down the pier checking the dark water with your light. The bottom was mostly dark grey mud and not much color existed until your light hit a lobster, which was bright red and orange. The moment they saw your light, their claws would come up in defense. It paid to be quick and not hesitate. The faster you could grab their head the easier it was getting them in the bag.

One day the master diver ran up to me and told me to grab a scuba team and get into the Boston Whaler. There was a bomb threat on the Coast Guard *Eagle*. The U.S. Coast Guard Academy was directly across the river from Groton Submarine Base, and the USCG *Eagle* was the Coast Guard's tall ship. It was 275-feet long, fifty years old and was a mascot for the Coast Guard. It was also used to train young officers at the academy.

Once the equipment and team were in the boat, the master diver stepped aboard, grabbed the controls, and drove the boat. He turned and looked at me and another diver and told us to get dressed. Looking for a mine is not rocket science. It's nothing more than a swim and if you have good visibility, it's an easy day.

However, finding a mine and removing it from a vessel is another story. Our method in those days was not to disarm it, but more like "snatch and run." We had a long brass cable with a loop on one end. Brass was used because it is non-magnetic and doesn't rust. We would lasso the device, then attach the end of the cable to a small boat, which would take off at high speed and snatch the device off the ship. Hopefully, the devise would be far enough away from the hull when it detonated to minimize damage to the target.

As the Boston Whaler pulled up to the pier at the Coast Guard Station, it was sheer pandemonium and chaos. Everyone was evacuating the ship and running down the pier when the USCG *Eagle*'s commanding officer ran up to us and ordered us to stand off for a safe period of time.

He explained the bomber called a second time and said the bomb was due to go off in fifteen minutes. He said he didn't want anyone to get hurt and to evacuate the area. The commanding officer then turned and ran off the pier to join his crew. The master diver maneuvered the Boston Whaler closer to the *Eagle*, and directed us to tie up to the pier, and shut the engines down. He turned to us and said get in and find it.

My dive partner protested, demanding that we take the captain's advice and wait a safe period. All the while they were arguing I sat there praying and got through two "Our Fathers" and was just completing my second "Hail Mary" when the master diver had enough and said, "Ricky, get in and find it."

Unleashed, I hit the water, completed my safety checks, and I was off. From the moment I left the surface, I positioned myself so I could see from the keel to the waterline. Since it was a tall ship, its draft was minimal. I swam as fast as I could up the starboard side and then down the portside moving counterclockwise.

It was the fastest 550-foot swim of my life. I surfaced under the dive boat and said, "All clear, Master Diver."

"You sure, Ricky," he replied. "That was pretty fast."

"Yes, Master Diver, all clear."

He told me to do it one more time. I smiled and said, "No problem."

The second time I scanned the hull I took my time to enjoy the scenery, and just like the first time the hull was clear. I surfaced and said it was all clear.

"Good job, Ricky." He and I then crawled up onto the pier and walked toward the captain and crew at the head of the pier. I couldn't have been prouder when the master diver said, "Ricky, give them the news," and I replied, "All clear, sir."

The Captain shook our hands and just said, "You guys are fucking nuts."

The trip back across the river was filled with emotions. On the one hand, the diver who refused to get in the water was quiet and embarrassed, while I was proud that I got the job done. But I was also sad, because the other diver was a friend and I knew his days as a Navy Diver were in jeopardy. I never saw him again after that job.

CHAPTER 9

DITCH WITCH

After a three-year tour at the Navy Submarine Support Facility in Groton, Connecticut, I reported to Charleston, South Carolina as a first-class petty officer and first-class diver. My job title assignment was leading petty officer.

I was once told at the beginning of my career that one day my leadership style would be the culmination of all the master divers that I ever worked for. When I met my next master diver (Gary), I had no idea how I would fit in with his grand plan. He asked me during my check in, "Petty Officer Bettua, are you a good diver?"

I thought to myself, *Is this a joke?* I was coming off diving 1,000 hours per year and probably had more time diving that year than all the divers stationed here combined. I replied, "Master Diver, I'm a great diver."

He went on to say that he knew that, but he needed more from me and explained soon that I would be running the whole show. I replied, "I'll do whatever you ask me to do."

Before I could take over as leading petty officer, I worked one month for the diver I would replace. He'd recently become a chief petty officer. I would like to say he assisted in creating a smooth turnover, but it was just the opposite. In that short period of time, he showed me everything I did not want to become in a leader.

I went to the master diver after a month and told him I had enough of the chief and was ready to assume the responsibility of Leading Petty Officer, and he agreed. I asked if he would give the chief an administrative position in the diving locker to keep him off the waterfront. I'd found that the morale was better on the boat without him.

I was used to the master diver and chiefs in Connecticut staying in the dive locker handling all the planning and scheduling, and the tedious work of dealing with quality assurance paperwork. But here at the Shore Intermediate Maintenance Activity (SIMA), the master diver went on every job, not to supervise and certainly not to dive, but he was there for me if I needed him. If things were not going right, he would take over and tell me to get dressed.

That was my job, to figure things out and get the job done when things were going wrong. After all my experiences over the past three years at Groton, I loved getting in the water and teaching the new kids the traits I had acquired.

But it wasn't long before I realized that things were going to get difficult and dangerous. The surface ship squadron decided to pass all the easy quick jobs over to the *Sierra* Dive Locker, while tasking us, the SIMA divers, with the more difficult jobs, since we had a much larger crew.

One of the most challenging jobs I faced was changing the propeller blades of ships *while* they are in the water. It had never been done before.

Most Navy combatant ships have a Controllable Reversable Pitch (CRP) system, which uses a hydraulic system to change the degree of pitch on the propeller blades from full ahead to full astern without changing the shaft speed. This makes the vessel highly maneuverable during combat situations. This system pumps oil down the shaft into the propeller hub to engage the blades and move them to the desired position.

Over time the propeller hub would start to leak oil and eventually the ship would have to go to drydock to have a series of O-rings replaced. It cost millions of dollars to put a Navy ship into drydock and take it out of service. We needed to figure a way to make the repair underwater.

I was invited, along with others, to help Naval Sea Systems Command (NAVSEA) engineers figure out if it could be done while the ship is waterborne. To do that, we first needed to go to school and learn how the job was done in drydock.

Each blade is held in place with eight MorGrip bolts, covered by caps. The bolts are pressurized to 40,000 psi which stretches them, and once stretched they go in and out easily when the pressure is released. After the bolts are removed, the blade is pulled out of the hub. This gives access to a massive plate that is then lifted out to gain access to the O-rings that need to be replaced.

What made the job seemingly impossible underwater was that you cannot allow saltwater to penetrate the hub as that would contaminate the entire system. No one knew how to overcome that problem. But sometimes bringing in new people to consider a problem can result in a viable solution. That's what happened in this case.

We suggested that in order to replace the O-rings in the water, we should rotate the hub down to the six o'clock position after the blades were removed, and then the hub should be pressurized. Oil is lighter than water and it would displace the seawater in the hub. So, we would jack the plate down on long studs, reach inside the oil-filled cavity to change the O-ring, then put it back together.

On one such underwater repair, I was assigned to remove the caps and the MorGrip bolts and prepare the blade for lifting out. We started using a three-foot-long breaker bar to remove the caps so we could reach the MorGrip bolts. The caps were incredibly tight and no amount of force would budge them.

We decided to use a hydraulic impact wrench to see if the caps could be loosened, but even with green divers helping by pushing on my back I couldn't keep the removal device from jumping off the caps. I asked a green diver to go get a line and when he returned, I had him tie me in close to the propeller.

Now I could push the impact diver into the caps using my chest and in doing so I could create much more force. As I squeezed the impact driver's control, the hydraulic wrench hammered away at the cap as I pushed down on the machine with my chest.

Suddenly, I was gasping for air. My heart was racing, and I couldn't catch my breath. I shouted to topside, exclaiming I couldn't breathe and my chest hurt. The green diver untied the rope and I was pulled up. As I clutched my chest on the surface, the master diver shouted for the team to get me out of the water. It looked as if I was having a heart attack.

I heard the siren of an ambulance, but our diving medical officer (DMO) arrived first at the scene. My helmet was removed and he quickly cut off my wetsuit to help him determine if I was having a heart attack.

Emergency medical techs arrived and hooked an EKG machine to my chest. My electro-cardio rhythm was erratic. The DMO asked the master diver what I was doing when it happened. When he heard that I'd been pushing on an impact wrench with my chest, he looked at me and said, "You dumb ass! You manually changed your cardiac rhythm by using your chest to push down on the wrench. Just calm down, breathe this oxygen for a while and you'll be fine."

Later that day, I was examined by a cardiologist, and after he examined the EKG results, he said, "Young man, nothing is wrong with your heart. In fact, it's one of the healthiest I've ever seen."

Our Oliver Hazard Perry class frigates started to develop the same leaking hub problem as their big sister Spruance class destroyers. The frigates are a small lightweight craft only 410-feet long that specialize in anti-submarine warfare. They are gas turbine powered, but with only a single propeller system. Prior to our involvement, all Perry class frigates were required to go into drydock to fix the issue. That was because there were no hawse pipes or pad eyes—devices welded to the hull of ships–directly above the propeller that we could use as braces for removing or installing blades.

As more and more frigates needed to head to drydock, pressure was applied on us to find a way we could do it in the water. We needed something to connect a multitude of chain falls, hoisting devices using chain to lift heavy objects, and come-a-longs, hand winches using cables to pull, tighten or straighten, to safely lift and replace the blade.

Together we all came up with the idea of using a single heavy wire with three unique grommets crimped in place. This would allow us to attach our main chain fall and two come-a-longs to the grommets. The wire would run completely around the ship and on the surface, we would have a twenty-ton chain fall to get the wire tight.

Once we showed everyone we could do it, we were labeled as the Navy's blade changing team and would go around the globe fixing frigates and destroyers that had either leaking hubs or damaged blades. The commanding officer loved us because we were making money for the command. If a ship was outside of our squadron's responsibility, that squadron would get a bill for our services. Money was flowing in because of our unique skillset.

Once we were sent into Israel to change out a destroyer's bent blade. A US submarine had damaged a blade on a Spruance class destroyer during a simple mooring exercise. Of course, working in a foreign port can present unique challenges. Even the simplest of things can become an issue. For example, the crane that was previously contracted to work with us was owned by someone of a different religious belief and therefore was not allowed in the port.

I needed to locate another crane suitable for our needs and carry cash for the arrangement. After trying several companies, I finally found one willing to work for us. The company demanded full payment in advance, which was a problem. The best terms I was willing to offer was fifty percent down and the balance paid when we were done in three days. After some haggling, a deal was struck.

The following morning, the crane arrived and was set up. It looked decrepit and at least fifty years old. On the first lift, the crane operator dropped the new blade as he was lifting it from the truck and it bounced on the pier. The captain of the ship came out in a huff, screaming that we damaged his new blade. The master diver just looked at him and said, "You don't own it yet, it's not yours until I put it on your ship! Now if you will excuse me, we have work to do."

There was nothing better in the Navy than being a master chief, which is the pinnacle of the enlisted ranks. Master chiefs comprise less than one percent of the total force in the military and it literally requires an act of Congress to reprimand one. You don't become a master chief by being a dumb ass and as such they can speak their mind to anyone. Master chief/master diver are even more rare, making up .001% of the Navy. But with their extreme specialization comes an innate amount of responsibility, which is shouldered by them alone.

I asked the master diver to go aboard one day while we were in Israel and find out if I made chief petty officer as I heard the list came out. He came back and said for us to put everything away, we were going out to celebrate Bettua's advancement to chief, and the next day we returned to Charleston.

We partied like rock stars in Israel that night and I even called my parents back in the States to tell them the good news. Later that night in the hotel the master chief was going into his room and I was going into mine next door and he said, "Ricky, you didn't make chief petty officer. I just didn't have the heart to tell you sober."

I was disappointed, of course, but I knew it was my own fault. I needed to complete my "Enlisted Surface Warfare Qualifications," but to do so required me to go back to sea. I was subdued on the flight to Charleston, but I vowed to make chief petty officer the following year. It would be the only time I did not advance at my earliest opportunity.

One of the last jobs I did while at SIMA Charleston was helping with a massive propeller change on a cruiser. Navy cruisers are 580-foot long, huge compared to a destroyer, and of course everything on them was extra-large. After weeks of planning, we were set up to start the job. The master diver wanted me to supervise the majority of the job, then I would handle the more complex parts, like taking the propeller off and gliding the new one back on.

It didn't matter the size of the ship; all propeller changes start the same. Take good measurements forward of propeller, remove pad eye plug, remove dunce cap, then break the boss nut free. Everything was going according to schedule and we were moving through each step very methodically.

Once the dunce cap was removed and the crane brought it to the surface, we marveled at the size of the cap. I remember someone saying, "Wow, how big is the nut going to be?" There's nothing difficult about breaking free a boss nut. All Navy boss nuts have a keeper that first needs to be removed. The nut itself, no matter how big, resembles a castle nut and the ship carries a special wrench with which to break it free.

The wrench fits over the nut and we use either a crane or a chain fall to begin moving it. Once the nut is broken free, it is easily rotated around the shaft by two divers. We then rig a boss nut catcher behind the shaft and simply unscrew the nut until it screws onto the boss nut catcher. In this case, the nut weighed nearly a ton. The system really is fool proof and very diver friendly, the only way for it not to work is if the divers are not paying attention.

Since I was the diving supervisor, I was wearing a headset to speak to the divers and every fifteen seconds I was asking the divers how the nut was moving and if it was threading onto the catcher, and over and over again the team confirmed all was going well, right up to the point when they reported: "Topside, we dropped the nut."

This nut is made when the ship is being built, and as you can imagine you can't just go to the local hardware store and buy a bronze nut that's five feet in diameter and weighs the same as a Toyota Corolla. This was an absolute cluster fuck and I looked over at the master diver who was with me in the pilot house and told him what happened.

He bolted up, Oreo cookies flying everywhere, and he shouted, "What do you mean they dropped the nut!"

"It's gone."

"Bring them up."

"Roger that, Master Diver."

Once both divers hit the surface and were un-hatted, the master diver got into their faces, shouting and cursing, and I didn't envy them one bit. After the barrage was over, we put our heads together on how to recover this nut.

I told everyone I had reached the bottom of the basin several times and explained that it consisted of ten feet of soup and then soft mud. Anything this heavy and dense would have sunk into the mud.

The master diver said, "Let's find out. Ricky, get dressed."

I was about to embark on a task that would ultimately lead me to see how far I was willing to push myself to complete a job to my satisfaction.

The plan was to hang a fifty-pound weight off the end of the shaft and follow the line down to see if the nut was there. Within minutes, I was in the water along with another diver. We set the line up as the master diver asked, then I began to follow it. From topside, I heard the master diver say, "Going down Red," and I replied, "Roger that!"

The bottom was just as I had described, and the weight had landed in a larger impression created by the massive nut. I pushed my arms into the thick mud up to my helmet but felt nothing. So, I returned to the surface. I explained the situation to the master diver, then we broke for the day so we could come up with a plan.

The master diver called around and the shipyard divers said they had an air vacuum that was twentyfeet long. An air vacuum has a nickname, "Ditch Witch," for its ability to move a large amount of mud, rock, or whatever happens to be in its way. It's a flexible tube six inches in diameter with a valve and air hose mounted on the diver's end. When the diver opens the valve, air is forced into the tube near the bottom side. As the air rises toward the surface, it expands causing a massive amount of lift that pulls in everything that fits into its mouth and drives it toward the surface.

The next morning a massive compressor was brought down to the pier to power the ditch witch and I was chosen to see if I could clear the mud and find the missing nut. The master diver would supervise and we would have three divers in the water. Two divers would stay at the top of the ditch witch, one would hold the ditch witch tube and the other would tend me, red diver.

Once I sat down on the bottom, the top of the ditch witch tube was about twenty feet above me. I was warned by the shipyard divers to watch my hands around the mouth of the ditch witch when it was operating as it could pick up a steel cannon ball. I stood up with the ditch witch tube steadied by both legs and opened the valve. This thing was like a vacuum on steroids and before I even knew it, I felt the walls of the tunnel on my upper arms. I was creating a three-foot wide tunnel and I was going down like I was on an elevator.

The whole time the master diver was checking on me as I sank deeper and deeper. I also could hear the other divers who were now on the bottom. The last thing I heard from them was the top of the ditch witch tube was now even with the bottom which meant I was twenty feet under the mud and approximately 70′ below the surface.

I felt the end of the witch hit something both solid and heavy and I squatted down. But before reaching my prize, I turned off the ditch witch because I didn't want to get hurt. I was standing on the nut and reached further down to feel the threads. I called up and said, "Topside red diver. I've got it."

I'd no sooner spoken when the tunnel collapsed. I heard the other team report. "Topside green, the tunnel collapsed. I repeat the tunnel collapsed." There I was seventy feet down with twenty feet of mud on top of me.

I didn't panic, in fact, it didn't initially register that I was in danger. But the moment the master diver spoke to me, I could tell he was concerned. "You okay, Ricky?"

"Yes, Master Diver, I'm okay, but I can't move."

It was as if I was in cement and my legs and arms–even my fingers—were frozen in place. The master diver's voice cracked, but he tried his best to remain calm. "Ricky, turn the witch back on."

"I can't move."

He then asked how far my hand was from the valve. "Not more than twenty inches."

In truth, I was never worried about my predicament. I wasn't hurt, I had plenty of air. I was just locked in mud. It never dawned on me that my dive table schedule for seventy feet was a maximum of fifty minutes and I would well exceed that and would require a decompression chamber. It also didn't occur to me that the longer I stayed here in the chilly mud unable to move, the colder I would become and exposure would soon become a factor.

Everything on the surface was absolute chaos as the master diver planned an all-out assault to get me out of that tunnel. He called all the other master divers in the area who brought their best divers. The plan was to use water pressure from the ship's fire main system to blow the mud out of the tunnel and hopefully I could be reached in time.

While their plan for a massive rescue team was coming together, I remained surprisingly calm and relaxed inside the collapsed tunnel. To some extent, I felt safe in my muddy hole like a mud-crab. I started moving one finger on my left hand, which was near my stomach, then I could move two fingers, and soon I was moving all four fingers, as if I was waving.

When you are focused on something meaningless like moving your fingers, your mind can start to wander. I was probably daydreaming about my boat, a beautiful twenty-five-foot Contender Center Console with twin two hundred horsepower outboards that I kept at my house in Charleston and hoping I would see it again soon. Meanwhile, my fingers kept going. Every five to ten minutes, the master diver would check on me and say help was coming and to hang in there. But now I was able to move my hand and I was reaching my fingers toward what I thought was the direction of the valve.

Now I was on a mission. My hand had enough movement and I was pushing forward toward the valve, but I was also getting cold, very cold. Every now and then I heard a loud boom, which was my air escaping the mud. It was a race against time, which I would experience many times to come in my life.

Finally, I reached the valve and exclaimed I was ready to turn the witch back on, I was shivering uncontrollably, which made talking difficult. The master diver and the team topside were set to put the rescue divers in the water to come get me, but I exclaimed I was not leaving that hole until a diver handed me a line to recover the nut.

The master diver said, "Ricky, don't worry about that. We need to get you out of the water. You have already omitted several hours of decompression and you must be freezing."

"Then a couple more minutes won't matter," I responded with my teeth chattering.

It was probably my father who instilled pride in me as a little boy by always saying to me, "If you are going to do a job, do it right the first time or don't do it at all." Now I had grown into a man and a senior Navy diver so I was not about to fail or ask anyone to do something that I could not. I would have preferred to die in the muddy tunnel than quit and put someone else's life at risk to complete what I had started.

The other team splashed down with a three-inch Kevlar Line and arrived on the bottom. I could hear them say they could not see the top of the ditch witch. Wherever I was, it was deeper than the twenty-foot-long tube. Finally, I heard what I was waiting for from the master diver. "Open the ditch witch."

"Yes, Master Diver."

He could tell I was shivering uncontrollably and upon opening the valve, it cleared all mud out of the collapsed tunnel in just minutes. One diver tended the other diver and before I knew it someone was tapping on my head to pass me the line. This time I kept the ditch witch on as I tied off the nut. After that, I crawled out of what would have been my muddy grave, and with the assistance of the other divers, I returned to the surface.

Once out of the water, un-hatted, and muddied from head to toe and shivering beyond belief, the master diver gave me a big hug, then I was rushed to the awaiting chamber to be treated for omitted decompression. I'd been in the water for three hours, two of them trapped under twenty feet of mud.

CHAPTER 10

BLOW AND GO

I remember when the diving detailer at the Pentagon asked me where I wanted to go next after my three-year tour in Charleston. That was 1989 and I was a first-class diver and first-class petty officer. I replied, "Master Diver, I am worldwide deployable. Send me to a ship anywhere that needs me." With that, I was sent to the USS *Orion* (AS-18), a submarine tender stationed in Sardinia, Italy.

I had to marvel at the wisdom of the detailer after I met the dive locker crew. I was one of nine first-class petty officers/first-class divers assigned to the *Orion*, but there was no chief and no master diver. Maybe the detailer had a crystal ball and knew I would become a chief. That was my immediate goal. Despite the ranking of the divers, the dive locker was a nightmare.

The day I reported aboard, I asked for my enlisted surface warfare qualification (ESWS) book. I had only about two months to complete it before I could be evaluated for chief petty officer. In a nutshell, I needed to learn as much as I possibly could about the ship, and for each required item I needed the signature of the related specialist.

I was way ahead of the game because at my first command I qualified in all positions in damage control. But it would be another race against time to get the final qualification before my screening for chief. I needed to be a chief because I was intent on taking charge of the dive locker and without that rank, the other divers would be difficult to manage.

Initially, I wanted nothing more than to get settled into my new home here, but good housing was in short supply and I was on a wait list. I could have just ignored the poor management and chaos in the dive locker and coasted behind everyone else until my housing was secured. But that only lasted a week and I couldn't stand it any longer. I asked the current leading petty officer to go with me and see the division officer. He had no idea why I wanted to talk to the division officer or why I asked him but he came along. He was in for a surprise.

The meeting lasted less than a minute as I told the division officer I was ready to take control of the dive locker, and immediately the current Leading Petty Officer objected profusely. The division officer asked me why he needed to grant my request, and I told him that the locker was "a complete cluster fuck from lack of leadership." Then he asked if I was a senior. "Yes, by years, sir," I replied. I had been a first-class diver and a first-class petty officer years longer than the current sailor.

"Okay, Petty Officer Bettua, you are the new Leading Petty Officer. Square it away." And with that, it was done. It was up to me to prepare for the new master diver, and also for me to become the chief. I called the divers together and let them know I was the new Leading Petty Officer and my style would be different from the last. "You can do what I ask and we can remain friends, or fuck the friendship, and you will do what I ask." Everyone understood and agreed.

A few short months later, I became a chief petty officer which to me was akin to being reborn. The moment I was advanced I was in a brotherhood of one hundred other chief petty officers aboard and that brotherhood was close. Everything instantly became easier because of my new rank and interacting with the other chiefs allowed me to build a dive crew that was second to none.

Everything now in the diving locker was in sync. I was the chief and I had my diving supervisors, and we had our divers just as it was meant to be. The day finally came and we received our own master diver. This was a good thing as it allowed me to be on the dive boat more and the master diver would take care of the immense number of meetings and the paperwork.

Every job completed by a diver on a Navy submarine has

quality assurance paperwork assigned to it, and we would have to sign off each step of the way as they were completed. So, working for a master diver shielded me from the responsibility of the paperwork and now I could turn out even more dive jobs.

This master diver was not like the others I'd worked for over the years. Rather than being brash and outspoken, he was meek and mild-mannered. That left people wondering who really was in charge. It didn't matter to me because I had the best of both worlds. I was a chief, but I could still dive and supervise down on the dive boat.

The *Orion* headed toward the eastern Mediterranean to provide submarine support off the coast of Egypt. We anchored in deep water amid rough seas with huge rollers. It took an entire day to get the ship on just the right mark, and after we were anchored, you could feel the ship pitching and rolling. It takes a lot to move a ship that weighs more than 9400 tons, but the ocean has no problem showing you who's boss.

Once anchored, tugs brought out four massive Yokohama rubber fenders to go between us and a two-hundred-foot barge that was now tied up alongside us. The seas, which were now ten to twelve feet, were moving the barge up and down effortlessly. All the while, we divers were watching the evolution and getting ready to dive the next day.

Our first job was with a 688-class submarine that needed to come alongside our ship for supplies and repairs. One of those repairs required my dive team to replace the submarine's missing anchor. Without an anchor, the submarine would need to stay at sea and could not pull into port or even get close to the coast.

Late in the afternoon we saw the 688 coming toward us and were watching as she prepared to tie up to the barge. It would be a challenge for any captain as the barge was pitching up and down. Submarines have a device called a secondary propulsion motor (SPM), which is lowered down and used for maneuvering at close quarters. The motor could swing 360 degrees providing thrust in any direction with a multidirectional propeller.

As the sub came alongside the barge, a mooring line was

passed over, but before it could be grabbed by the sailors on the barge it fell into the water. That line then went right into the thrusting motor, which was keeping the submarine in place, and the motor seized it up. The submarine had no choice but to do an emergency break away from the barge in order to bring its bow back into the large swells. Now she was limping away with no anchor, no Secondary Propulsion Motor, and dragging three hundred feet of mooring line, which could foul the sub's propeller.

The master diver and I were summoned to the bridge where the commodore, captain, and repair officer were present. I could see the floundering 688 class submarine was 500 yards off our port bow and was having difficulties keeping her bow into the seas. In a huff, the commodore asked if we could dive on a lit off submarine that was underway and not tagged out. The master diver deferred to me since I was a 688-class submarine expert.

"Chief, what do you think?"

I explained there were too many obstacles and the possibility of lives being lost would be greatly enhanced. The commodore then pointed out that there were a hundred sailors on that sub whose lives were in jeopardy now.

I said that technically and legally we couldn't dive on the sub, but with the right divers and a fair amount of luck, it might be possible.

"Get it done, Chief Bettua. God be with you," the commodore said.

The plan was for the ship to set our rigid inflatable boat (RIB) into the water with just two of us onboard. I had gone to the Nova Marine Boat Factory myself and overseen the construction of the boat and had them build it as solid as they could. I was counting on the quality of that construction now.

I would pull around to the barge and pick up the other divers and equipment. The seas now were twelve feet and the moment the RIB touched the water the swell receded twenty-four feet under us. But before the next swell could slam us, we started the boat, and disconnected the RIB from the three-point sling holding it up and dropped twenty feet to the ocean.

I had two great first-class divers, Gary and Jim, but I couldn't dive them together as I needed one of them to be standby diver. I had a young energetic diving corpsman (medic) named Frankie dive with Gary. Jim, who would later in his career become a master diver, was my standby diver. The entire ship watched us on every deck level as I came along the side the barge and one by one the divers and gear were passed over.

Once away from the pitching barge, we got the gear ready and I slowed to brief everyone. This would be the most dangerous job I'd ever attempted to date. I told everyone the propeller will be on the jacking gear at twelve revolutions per minute to hold the subs nose into the seas.

"Everything is lit off, including the ship's main seawater pump, which will kill you should you not do exactly what I say. I will bump the rudder and you will go off the forward part of this boat. You will then leave the surface and go to the stern plane together. Once on the stern plane, swim forward to the front of the plane, go under, then go to the 6 o'clock position. You must stay at 6 o'clock. Your life depends on it."

I paused to make sure they understood me, then continued. "Swim forward at 6 o'clock to the Secondary Propulsion Motor. Cut the line out but keep your hands out from it unless you want to lose them. Once the line is clear hold on to the line and take it down to at least forty feet, and as the submarine passes, let go, ascend, and I will pick you up behind the sub."

I looked at Gary and said, "You are responsible for Frankie. Do you understand me?"

"Roger that, Chief," he replied.

We pulled up to the submarine's conning tower, which was rolling back and forth from the swells, and huge waves were breaking over top of the sub. I drove the RIB as close as I dared before calling up to the sub's captain. He responded, "Nothing is tagged out, Chief."

I yelled back up to him and said, "I need your jacking gear engaged, the Secondary Propulsion Motor shut down, and your word you will not change those conditions." He agreed but said the main seawater pump was running to cool off the reactor. "We know," I said. The grate of the main seawater pump was about four feet in diameter and sucked in so much water to cool the reactor that if a diver got too close it would pin him to the grate and the suction would kill him.

His last words were: "You guys are fucking crazy!"

There was no chatter in the boat. We all knew the risk involved. Now the submarine's jacking gear was engaged, and as the submarine pitched up and down the propeller was coming out of the water. My plan would only work if I got the divers dangerously close to that propeller. They were ready to splash on the front of the boat. I waited and watched the rhythm of the ocean swells, moving the boat between the propeller and rudder. I bumped the rudder, which on a sub is both below and above the stern, and the divers were gone in an instant. The planes on the submarine, where the divers were headed, were like wings that extended out from the body of the sub.

Ten minutes felt like an eternity and I didn't know if my plan worked or, because of my command, I would lose two very good friends. Then they popped up behind the submarine about fifty yards out and I was flush with emotions. I gathered the divers who explained everything went like clockwork and the Secondary Propulsion Motor was clear of all line. I ran the boat back up to the conning tower and told the captain they were clean and clear.

It was getting late and the sun was about to set so the sub headed out to deep water where they could submerge and we returned to the ship. I used the radio in the boat to call the bridge and reported, "Job complete," and requested help on the barge to remove some of the gear and personnel. The officers on the bridge were so elated that we had cleared the sub they sent an entire department to our aid. I didn't envy the young guys getting off the boat, but just like spry little monkeys, they made it look easy. I would keep Gary and Jim in the boat to help me clip into the crane with our boat sling and get hoisted aboard the ship.

Our three-point sling was made of Kevlar and rated for five times the weight of our boat. It seemed like our entire crew was watching as I pulled around and got the RIB into position. The ship made sure to compensate for the swells and dropped down enough wire for Jim and Gary to make the connection quickly.

All the while I kept the boat in the right location. The moment the swell receded and the wire and sling were taut, we were knocked to the deck. Then, before the crane could pull us up, another swell lifted us up. The wire went slack and when that wave receded, the boat came down with a crack.

The forward leg of the sling broke and now the boat was hanging by the stern and we were clinging on for dear life. We shouted for the crane to drop us back down, but before they could react, the next swell arrived and the bow came up out of control. We quickly released the two rear legs of the sling and I started the engine. I pulled away from the ship and we all caught our breath.

The captain radioed us, asking if we were all okay. I said we were, then asked for two monkey lines to be dropped from the ship's boom. Jim and Gary would climb up the lines and board the ship. I would shed some weight and bring the RIB up myself in a cargo net. With Jim and Gary safely aboard, I guided the RIB into two suspended cargo nets and was swiftly raised aboard.

Years later, after I became a master diver, I had the pleasure of meeting the commanding officer of that 688 sub that we saved off the coast of Egypt, and he personally thanked me for our efforts and saving his career.

Upon returning home to La Maddalena, Sardinia, the *Orion* moored at its normal berth. The day was extremely windy and gusts were coming across the bay at forty knots. It took several Navy tugs to hold the *Orion* in place, while the ship attempted to moor on a small t-pier. The wind pushed the ship around and our captain felt the forward anchor chain might've been damaged. So, he wanted us to inspect it as soon as possible.

The three-inch chain stretched over four hundred yards and went down one hundred and ninety feet. As we watched everyone leaving the ship to go home to their families after being gone for two months, we got ready to dive. This job was somewhat technical because of the length of the anchor and the depth. The maximum time allowed at a hundred ninety feet was just five minutes.

The bottom time starts the moment you leave the surface to the moment you depart from the bottom. The only way you could exceed that 190/5 table was if you had a recompression chamber on station and you have approval from the commanding officer. The master diver asked me if I could swim it in less than five minutes, and my answer was no but under ten minutes.

I knew how fast I could swim a thousand yards, but with the added weight of twin tanks and the effects of nitrogen narcosis, I would be slowed down. Nitrogen narcosis is an anesthetic effect caused by nitrogen at extreme depths that is akin to having several stiff drinks. The master diver and I went to the commanding officer to brief him on the job and get permission to exceed the Navy's no-decompression tables. I was a bit of a golden boy after the recent submarine rescue, and he slapped me on the back and said, "I believe you can do anything you put your mind to, Chief. Get it done."

Although technically this was a very easy dive job and it would be over in fewer than ten minutes, I would learn a valuable lesson to never underestimate any job underwater ever again. The water clarity was easily one hundred and fifty feet and it would be nothing more than an all-out swim. I would dive out of the Rigid Inflatable Boat and the recall method would be an M-80 underwater explosive device. You could hear this thing underwater from a mile away should the boat want me to return to the surface.

As the boat moved out in front of the *Orion*, the standby diver and I were getting dressed for the dive and everyone was relaxed and laughing. All the married guys were pleading with me to get this done fast so they could get home to see their wives. The master diver checked and rechecked my air supply while I just sat there with a big smile on my face. On my arm I wore a white board where I had written the table and schedule for depths and times of 180/10, 190/10 and 200/10 and the decompression time for each. But I was sure I could swim the four hundred yards in less than the ten minutes allowed.

The master diver gave me two pats on the head and I slid into the cold water and completed my in-water checks. With an okay to the master diver I heard him say, "Red diver leaving the surface," and I was gone. Just like in second-class dive school, go means go, and there is absolutely no benefit to going down slowly so I swam just as fast as I could descending along the length of the chain. This chain was three inches in diameter and each link was at least twenty-four inches long and weighed close to two hundred pounds. So, it was easy to see and inspect as I swam over it.

After reaching a depth of more than 150 feet, I felt the toxic nitrogen making me feel a little lightheaded and the harder I swam, the harder I was breathing. That meant I was taking on even more nitrogen, compounding the issue. I was at a depth of about 180 feet when I heard a loud boom, and at first I thought the master diver had tossed an M-80 in the water to recall me. Then something caught my eye below me as it fluttered down to the bottom.

I swam down and picked it up off the bottom only to discover it was a submersible pressure and depth gauge and the depth gauge read 195 feet. Because of the effects of nitrogen narcosis and my mind moving slowly my eyes then went to the pressure gauge which read ZERO. This took a second or two to register in my brain then I reached back to feel for my submersible pressure gauge and depth gauge and found nothing more than an empty hose with air pouring out the end.

The air flowing out the end of the hose was high pressure air and even though I tried to crimp the hose I could do nothing to even slow it down. The nature and design of all scuba regulators is the air will flow toward the least amount of resistance and now that was the end of the hose and not my mouth. Being down almost 200 feet with little or no air by yourself is not a place you want to be, and it was time to go!

As I left the bottom, the visibility was so good I could see the dive boat above me but I was a long way from home. I had to forcefully suck the air through my second stage regulator as my precious air supply was free flowing out the end of the hose and to the surface. It was so hard to breathe I thought I was going to pass out and I finally reached up and removed my regulator. Now it was time to just blow and go.

I was at about a hundred feet and I could see standby diver

was in the water and kicking toward me as fast as he could, pulling another set of scuba. I had one hand over my head and I was steadily exhaling trying to get to him as quickly as I could. At sixty feet he met me and shoved the fresh regulator into my mouth and I took a minute to catch my breath.

I told myself to "just breathe" as I held onto the standby diver. Once I calmed down, we moved up to ten feet for me to decompress. Upon reaching the surface the master diver said he knew something was wrong the moment my air bubbles looked like a submarine was venting underwater. He asked what happened and I held up the hose with no submersible pressure gauge on it and said equipment malfunction.

"That's got to be a first," he said. "I'm glad it was you, Chief, and not one of the younger guys."

"Job complete," I said. "Let's get these horny guys home to their wives."

That would be the last time during my career that I would ever scuba dive without a partner.

CHAPTER 11

HOME OF THE TIGER

In January of 1991, I was one of four first-class divers invited to attend the Navy's eight-week Master Diver Evaluations in Panama City Beach. Each day the four of us would take a first-class diver class to sea with about twenty-four divers and supervise dives that would include real-life emergency scenarios. We were then graded on our performance and leadership while handling the situation.

My previous master diver's advice for becoming a master diver was that repetition creates perfection. I took his comment seriously and spent a month prior to the evaluation at a secluded rented beach house. Every day I went for a run and work out to get my head straight. Then I practiced supervising dives out loud for six hours. There are 136 line items or sentences you must say while running a normal surface supplied dive. I practiced saying them in order every day for a month.

At that time, the percentage of prospective candidates who would pass the course and get voted in by the sitting master divers was twenty-five percent. That meant that, in all likelihood, only one of us in our class would make it.

During the last week of the evaluation process, master divers from all over the world converged on Panama City to evaluate our performances. My three classmates all carried a clipboard so they wouldn't forget anything on their pre-dive checks or during the dive brief itself. Since I'd spent that extra month repetitiously going over dive after dive, I didn't need a clipboard, but I did need something to calm my nerves so my hands would not fidget. So, I laminated a large yellow smiley face on to a clipboard and wrote in big letters "Rick, just have Fun."

On the first day I was last out of the gate; the fleet of master divers had already watched and graded my classmates and now it was my turn. I stood up in front of the dive team and master divers and started to brief them, but I could see the master divers were wondering what was in my hand and why was I not reading notes from my clip board. The school's master diver who was assigned to us and had been with us the past seven weeks said, "Just watch. He doesn't need one." Five days later, I was the US Navy's newest and youngest master diver at age twenty-eight.

Being only a chief petty officer in rank but qualifying as a master diver put me at a huge disadvantage as there were many senior chief petty officers who were only first-class divers. That situation is like oil and water if the senior chief doesn't know his place. In Navy diving, the senior qualified diver is in charge, regardless of rank, which meant if there was a senior chief at my next command, they would be working for me as a chief. The diving detailer was looking after my best interest and stashed me at a small diving command back in Groton, Connecticut. His thought was to put me at Groton until I advanced to senior chief before sending me out to a major sea command.

However, upon arrival at my new command, I was greeted by not only one, but two senior chiefs. One came straight out and said he had no problem working for me while the other had some notion I would be working for him. The situation was rectified with a single phone call to the master chief/master diver detailer. I told him that this senior chief had a problem working for me. The very next day that senior chief received a set of orders to report to an ARS (Diving Rescue and Salvage) ship in Norfolk, Virginia working for a master chief/master diver.

One year later, that same diver detailer called me first and said, "Congratulations, Ricky, you're a senior chief. Pack your bags." Unbeknownst to me this arrangement was decided the day I became a master diver. There was an ARS out in the Pacific that was plagued with leadership problems and the detailer

promised the commanding officer that he would send me to the
ship as soon as I became a senior chief.

I asked the detailer where I was heading and he said USS
Salvor ARS-52. I quickly responded "I have one request, Master
Chief. I want to go through the senior enlisted academy."

He told me to wait one minute. The detailer walked down
the hall and into the office of the master chief petty officer of
the Navy (MCPON) and told him the situation. He came back
on the phone and told me to report to the U.S. Navy Senior
Enlisted Academy on Monday. The detailer said I would be the
first master diver and one of the youngest Senior Chiefs ever to
attend.

The average age of the students at the academy was forty-
two years old and I was only thirty. So, I suffered constant jokes
about being a young pup. During that period however, the Navy
instituted the Physical Readiness Test, which was nothing more
than an easy physical fitness test.

Many of my fellow senior chiefs in my class were struggling
to stay fit, so I started working them out every morning at 0500
before class to help. In doing so, they all ensured my homework
assignments were above reproach and I graduated with honors,
thanks to them.

Prior to reporting to my new command, I needed to burn
some leave time. The Navy only allows you to carry up to sixty
days. I was over and needed to use it or lose it. It had been
years since I spearfished because of my career, and I very much
wanted to get back to it. So, I decided to visit a local spearfishing
shop in Honolulu. That is where I met Tim, who would end up
being a lifelong friend.

Tim was college-educated but worked in the shop because
he loved spearfishing so much and it wasn't long before we
would be spearfishing together. Tim was a natural waterman
who could do it all, kayak, surf, and spearfish while the only
thing I had going for me was I could swim.

One day after a dive, Tim told me his boss and some friends
were going down to the Revillagigedo Islands three hundred
miles west of Cabo San Lucas, Mexico. I asked why and he said
they were going to shoot massive yellowfin tuna and wahoo

and that sounded amazing to me. I asked him if there were any spots available on the trip, but he said they had their own crew and they only went once a year. Two days later, Tim's boss, Brian, called me and said someone backed out and asked if I would like to go. He also told me how much it cost and what to bring. Over the next few weeks, I acquired all the gear I needed, including a custom speargun large enough for spearing huge fish weighing more than I weighed.

With all the gear on hand we all converged upon Cabo San Lucas, including a few divers who came down from California. We all met at the airport, had a drink, and I was introduced to everyone. Then we headed directly to the boat. Our hosts, Mike and Miss Sherry, owned and operated a world-class eighty-foot motor yacht built for spearfishing expeditions. We all stowed our gear and then the captain went over the safety equipment on the boat, explaining all the dos and don'ts.

It was obvious once you stepped on Captain Mike's boat, he had great pride in his vessel and was very meticulous in its care. Miss Sherry, for her part, was a master chef and you could always smell something yummy baking away in the galley. That night we all went out to a great Mexican restaurant and during dinner I listened to stories from previous trips out to the islands of San Benedicto, Roca Partida, and Socorro. The stories also described the number and size of sharks. I was quiet during dinner and was starting to get nervous and second-guess myself. Had I bitten off more than I could chew, so to speak?

The next day the diesels roared to life bright and early and I got up to see if I could give Capt. Mike a hand. Onboard we also had two Mexican deckhands who knew the routine quite well and before I knew it, we were underway. Miss Sherry brought Capt. Mike and myself a cup of coffee in the pilot house and Capt. Mike asked me what my background was. I explained to him I had been spearfishing over twenty years and was also a Navy master diver. He looked at me and said, "You're a sailor? Hey, would you mind relieving me at the helm for a few hours this evening?"

I smiled and said no problem.

He asked what experience I had in blue water spearfishing,

and I told him that I had never done it before but had been looking forward to it for a few years. He looked at me with eyes wide and said, "You better be a fast learner. The place we are going to can be very unforgiving."

Blue water is the water beyond the reef where pelagic fish roam. It has no bottom which can be seen only blue water and darker blue underneath you. Your depth perception is always off because you have no reference only shades of blue.

The rest of the team knew the transit would take all day to get there so they took their time getting up and several of them were seasick. Funny watching people who worked on shore trying to walk around a moving boat at sea, but the captain, Miss Sherry, and I were all used to it. I tried to be as helpful as possible, but when you're seasick you just want to be left alone.

Later in the afternoon we got together to talk about plans for the following day. I told everyone at the meeting I had absolutely no experience in blue water spearfishing. They put me at ease straight away and instead of making fun of me said I would be paired up with a national spearfishing champion. Gerald was a gifted mentor for me, soft spoken and patient. He never got loud or excited or upset. He explained from his point of view that blue water spearfishing was the easiest of all types of diving and being as I was diving in Hawaii this would be much easier. Then there was a conversation which I paid very close attention to and that was about sharks.

I think it was Brian who told me not to swim alone. "If Gerald shoots a fish and you cannot keep up with him, then swim to the closest set of divers." I nodded in agreement. I was told there are many sharks, but they keep their distance and normally stay down forty to fifty feet below. I was specifically told to watch for any shark on the surface as they were desperate and would be more aggressive. Later, they said if I saw a tiger shark to signal the boat and get out of the water immediately.

All night I was on edge and couldn't sleep. I never felt like this on any Navy job and I knew deep down I was nervous. About 3 a.m., I felt the boat moving from the rough channel into the smooth waters behind the lee of the island. The captain then dropped the anchor and shut the diesel engines down. Now it was peaceful and the next couple hours I fell into a deep sleep.

I heard people rising and walked up to the main deck to have a look. The island was very tall and volcanic. It looked like grey ash with only a few sparce bushes here and there. The bay where we were anchored was glass calm and the deepest shade of blue that can be imagined. In the far corner of the bay was a small sailboat. Capt. Mike, who now was standing by my side, pointed at the craft and asked, "Do you know the writer, Carlos Eyles? He wrote the book, *Last of the Bluewater Hunters*. When I said I knew the book, Mike said Eyles was on that boat and would be having dinner with us later that night.

Miss Sherry already had breakfast laid out for us, but everyone was excited to get in the water. Gerald looked at me and said let's take our time. So, we enjoyed Miss Sherry's first full breakfast onboard. Gerald explained that unlike other places, the fish could be here any time of the day, so there was no need for us to rush.

Gerald had been to San Benedicto many times before and he explained to me the captain had anchored us on the best spot, which was a pinnacle that came up to ninety feet below us. We walked up and looked at the depth sounder in the pilot house and it was full of baitfish. Capt. Mike asked what our plan was and Gerald said we were going to dive right there. Mike agreed that was a great idea and said he would be moving the boat about a half mile to the west.

We got ready to slip into the water and Gerald explained for me to watch what he did. He would dive down just thirty feet and wait amongst the baitfish for about a minute and a half before returning to the surface. I understood and we both slipped into the blue water. The water was alive with thousands and thousands of blue and gold fusiliers.

We waited for Capt. Mike to pick up the anchor and move off before we started diving. I saw the next closest set of divers about three hundred yards away. We got into a rhythm where Gerald would go down and when he returned to the surface, I would repeat his actions.

We were diving less than an hour and while I was on the surface, I saw a school of tuna coming our way. What an amazing sight, about fifteen fish, all of them as big as a small car. Larger tuna will always draft off their smaller counterparts to use less energy. Gerald waited for the smaller fish to go by and picked out one of the biggest in the rear.

I heard the shaft impact the fish with a loud CRACK and in a fraction of a second it raced off towing my new dive partner. I felt secure and safe where I was because I could see the bottom ninety feet below and the blue and gold fusiliers were keeping me company. But being a military man, I take orders well and one of those orders was for me not to swim alone. I picked my head up out of the water and saw Gerald was further than the next set of divers, so I started to swim in their direction.

No longer able to see the bottom or the friendly fusiliers, it was just blue everywhere I looked. Occasionally, a shark swam by, but they were down forty feet or so and minding their own business. They were whaler sharks between six and eight feet long. As I swam at a moderate pace, but with a purpose, I noticed I was not getting closer to the other divers.

I saw the panga (small boat) going out to get Gerald and his tuna. I kept swimming, but now with a bit more force to get closer to the other divers. I started to feel uneasy but couldn't figure out why. The ocean was flat calm and the water was crystal clear with only a small whaler in my view every few minutes. But something was wrong. It was as if the hair on the back of my neck was standing straight up as a warning.

I looked out in front of me, then to the left, then to the right. Nothing. Yet, something was wrong. Then I turned to look behind me and saw a massive shark swimming just below my float which was only seventy-five feet behind me. The shark was sixteen to seventeen feet long and looked like it was over four feet wide. It saw me and started to swim toward me slowly.

My mind was racing and everything was in ultraslow motion. *What do I do? What do I do?* As the shark got closer, I could clearly see it had large stripes on her side. *Shit, an adult tiger shark!* Now she was on the surface and I peered above the water and saw that her dorsal fin, which was three-feet tall was coming straight for me. I remembered what Brian said: If a shark is on the surface, it is desperate and if it's a tiger call the boat. I tried to scream, but very little came out.

I brought my fins down to make myself look as large as possible, but to no avail. She continued her trek directly toward me. The right side of my brain was screaming at me to shoot it, and the left side of my brain was shouting for me to bump it. The left side of my brain was saying the other divers will laugh at me if I shoot it. So, I decided to bump it, but bump it good. The right side of my brain kept screaming at me to shoot it. *Shoot it now, Rick!*

I waited too long and now the massive beast was upon me and when there was only three to four feet between us, she opened her mouth. I swear it looked as if I could crawl inside it was so large and I even saw the ridges on the roof of her mouth. Now she was too close for me to shoot and at the last second the left side of my brain won the argument. I lifted all sixteen pounds of my speargun high over my head out of the water and in one swift but violent motion it came down directly into her right eye! The massive shark, in an attempt to get away from the pain, turned on a dime to flee and in doing so its tail lifted me out of the water and my head came crashing down into the side of the panga.

The Mexican deck hands and Gerald saw everything and the Mexicans were shouting for everyone to get out of the water. "Casa el tigre!" (home of the tiger). Gerald asked over and over if I was okay, but I was in a fog and couldn't answer. Upon returning to the Ambar, I noticed my gun was still loaded and unloaded it on the swim platform. All the while the Mexicans were shouting and Gerald was trying to explain to Capt. Mike and Miss Sherry what I just experienced.

I didn't say a word to anyone. I took my wetsuit off and walked silently down below to my stateroom, then crawled into my bed. It would be the first time in my life I experienced shock. Yet no one recognized the symptoms at the time.

I spent the entire afternoon locked away in my stateroom in fear. Later that evening, when Carlos Eyles came over for dinner, Capt. Mike explained to him what happened with the tiger shark and that I spent the entire afternoon in my stateroom. Carlos recognized the symptoms straight away, and he and

Capt. Mike came down to my stateroom with a glass of vodka to coax me out.

I came up to the salon and all the divers were there and Carlos asked if I would tell the story. We all sat down and I told them everything. I explained that I am very good with orders and you gave me two rules to follow, don't swim alone and if I saw a tiger shark to call the boat and I did.

Then I told them about the argument in my mind to bump it or shoot it and I was confused which to do because I didn't want them laughing at me. So, I decided to bump it as it was coming in for a bite. I explained that I raised my gun as far out of the water as I could before bringing it down into her right eye while she was attempting to take a bite.

They all said, "Rick, you should have shot it. Don't ever let a tiger shark get that close to you. Shoot it next time." With that, they all gave me a pat on the back and Capt. Mike made some comment about "balls of steel" in a toast and we shared a beautiful spaghetti dinner with our guest Carlos.

There's a Chinese proverb that states if you can survive a life-threatening experience, you will be gifted by boundless good luck. The very next day I shot my first blue water fish, a yellowfin tuna weighing 165 pounds. Then the following day, I shot another one that was 206 pounds, and on the third day yet another that weighed 185 pounds. I had beginner's luck the entire trip, and also got to make some great friends.

CHAPTER 12

PASS ME A MASK

As I walked aboard the USS *Salvor* for the first time, the captain and executive officer met me on the quarter deck and invited me to the wardroom for a chat and a cup of coffee. They explained to me that the previous leaders onboard made poor choices and many of them were recently fired. I assured them I would do my best not to disappoint anyone.

The captain nodded in approval, then said: "Master Diver, I fully intend on loading you up with as many duties as you can handle. In fact, I will continue to do so until you say enough."

"Roger that, sir," I answered.

"Your duties as a master diver onboard are miniscule in comparison to being the senior enlisted advisor or command senior chief," the captain continued. "There are one hundred and ten sailors onboard—thirty women and eighty men—that need leadership and guidance, and that will be your main focus. In addition, this ship needs you to become a command master chief as quickly as possible. Therefore, I want you to qualify as an officer of the deck so you can go the watch bill. It will help your future advancement." The watch bill is the list of officers available to stand watch.

I loved every aspect of my life onboard the *Salvor* and had no problem wearing many hats. Besides all the responsibilities the captain had given me, under his guidance, I was able to qualify as officer of the deck. This qualification, which is usually reserved for officers only, entails learning navigation and ship handling. Once I was qualified, I was in charge of the safe navigation of the ship when the captain was not on the bridge. It is the highest at-sea qualification attainable.

I enjoyed standing watch on the bridge especially at night which was usually quiet and peaceful. I would walk out onto the wing and look down onto the ocean as the ship's bow was cutting through the waves and would be mesmerized by the phosphorescence lighting up the sea as we passed. The luminous glow in the water is emanated from millions of tiny marine organisms and is most frequently seen in tropical seas.

Our first big mission was to steam from Hawaii to San Diego, then down to the Panama Canal to pick up a nuclear submarine and deliver it to Bremerton, Washington. This would take us weeks at sea and I was looking forward to getting underway. The *Salvor* was not a large ship. In fact, it barely classified as a ship at all at only 255 feet long and 51 feet wide. She resembled a large ocean tug with its massive forty-ton boom on the fantail. She was built as a workhorse for diving, rescue, salvage and towing operations and she was fitted with two automatic towing machines.

Just prior to leaving on our trip, I gathered the whole crew for a morale and welfare chat. After discussing our trip to Panama, I asked if there was anything we as a command could do to make the cruise better. Hands went up in an instant, the men asked if they could forego shaving while at sea. I said okay to that. Next, the women said if the guys aren't going to shave, then they should be able to wear their hair down. I had to think on that one but decided fair is fair. I said okay, but not in the engine room or around any operating machinery. Lastly, they all asked if I could come up with a relaxed uniform to wear while we were underway, which ended up being a command t-shirt with our logo on it and shorts.

The worst part about getting underway for weeks on end is the first three days. Everyone is cranky and they don't have their sea legs yet and of course most are missing their families. But after those initial days everyone settles into a rhythm, which then becomes a routine and everyone on the ship is in step. Days turn into weeks and before you know it, you're at your destination.

San Diego would be our last safe port for six weeks before

we returned here, but it turned out to be the doorway to a very *unsafe* destination for two crew members. The ship needed to refuel and replenish supplies in San Diego since our next leg was quite a bit farther than our first leg from Hawaii. Once we arrived, the crew were excited about receiving a few days of liberty. Before the captain released the crew, a crew member asked if they were allowed to visit Tijuana Mexico, which was just over the border a few miles away.

The captain asked me what I thought, and I said, "No, sir. I don't recommend it." Being a good leader means you are entrusted with making difficult decisions, some of which will not be popular. Concede where you can, but stand firm when you believe in your convictions, especially when it comes to safety.

In this instance, the captain overruled my decision, and said he didn't see any harm in it. "Master Diver, let them go."

"Roger that, sir," I answered. Although I supported the captain's decision, deep down inside I knew something bad could happen. As the command senior chief, it was not prudent to hang out with or fraternize with anyone junior than myself so that evening I went to dinner and then to the movies by myself. I got back to the ship about 11 p.m. and as I was crossing the ship's quarterdeck the phone rang and it was a hospital in Tijuana and they asked to speak to me. I answered and was told two of my shipmates were severely beaten, one had been stabbed multiple times and the other had a screwdriver sticking out the side of his head.

As a result of the brutal incident both sailors were released from military service and medically discharged. The ship was underway for Panama the next day and the captain requested my presence on the bridge. I found him sitting in his chair out on the wing in deep thought and said good morning to him. He just looked at me and said, "Never again will I overrule you in regard to the well-being of the crew. You were right, Master Diver". I told him when I was a young diver, a very wise master chief/master diver once told me, "Son, if it don't feel right, it ain't right," and that was why I had advised him the way I did.

We arrived at the Panama Canal and moored across the pier

from USS *Bolster*, which was to tow the second submarine, and we would have a combatant ship as an escort. The submarine to be towed was directly astern from us and I went over and started to inspect her.

When a submarine is towed, it has a nose cone fitted around her sonar dome that is then welded to the submarine at four points: 3, 6, 9 and 12 o'clock position. Four massive I-beams come together on the tip of the nose to a single pad eye. As a safety precaution, the pad eye is fitted with a 1 5/8" inch safety shackle that is to be the weak link in the towing arrangement.

Later that evening both ships had a joint barbeque on the pier and our crews got to mingle. I was introduced to the USS *Bolster*'s captain by my own captain and when I asked who her master diver was, I was surprised to find out she had no master diver onboard. This was highly irregular that a salvage ship would get underway for a towing mission without a towing expert onboard, but she assured me her team was ready for the task. She then asked if I had any pointers or if there was something to pay particular attention to, and I replied, "Change the 1 5/8-inch safety shackle for a 2-inch safety shackle." My captain even said, "You better listen to him." She disagreed and said she would be using the prescribed shackle.

The following morning *Bolster* was to get underway first and in doing so would require the assistance of four tugs. Being as the submarine was already hooked into the ship via the towing hawser—a thick cable attached from the ship to the bow of the submarine—two tugs would be required for each side to safely maneuver the ship out into the canal. My captain asked me if I would go out with the rigid Inflatable boat and film the evolution for training purposes.

I grabbed two divers to go with me and the deck department lowered the boat into the water and we were underway. It takes quite a bit of precise maneuvering on the part of the tug pilots to get the ship and submarine, which are tied to one another, safely out into the channel and pointing in the right direction.

We were just off the port side of *Bolster* filming when it became apparent that the ship was having difficulties lining up. In fact, she was ninety degrees to the bow of the submarine. She would need to use her engines to twist the ship to line up with the sub.

I'm not sure what happened on the bridge or what commands were given, but she backed very quickly and in doing so she put a massive load on the pad eye holding the chain stopper and the fourteen-inch nylon line went onboard. The pad eye took the load side on and was ripped from the deck and with it the chain and an experimental hawser went overboard.

On the *Salvor*, our towing wire was connected directly to 180 feet of chain and then connect to the two-inch safety shackle. But *Bolster* was using ninety feet of chain coupled to an experimental fourteen-inch nylon hawser as a shock absorber, which was connected to her towing wire.

As *Bolster*'s hawser tumbled into the water, it fell into the port propeller, and was now stretched tight. We stopped filming and slowly crept up to *Bolster*'s stern where I reached over to feel how tight the hawser had become. It was so tight if felt as if the nylon was now steel. The captain of the *Bolster* looked down on us from the fantail, and asked: "Master Diver, where does that line go?"

I answered that it appeared to be going into the port propeller. She then asked, "Are you sure?"

"Drop a mask down, ma'am, and I will confirm." I was wearing my khaki uniform and a pair of Danner boots when the mask was dropped down. I looked up at the ship's captain and said, "Ma'am, do I have your word you will not move anything?"

"Of course."

The ship and the submarine were being held in the center of the Panama Canal by four tugs; all of them were underway. I put the mask on, slipped into the water, took three good breaths held my breath, then pulled myself down along the stretched hawser under the ship to the port propeller. I counted at least a dozen wraps of the hawser around the forward part of the propeller and noticed the rope guard was crushed.

To return to the surface, I had to pull myself up, since I wasn't wearing fins. As soon as I came up, the tactical officer in command, who was on the front of the submarine, shouted for me to get out of the water. I climbed back into the boat and explained to the captain what I saw. I knew that *Bolster* would have to disconnect and pull back into the pier for repairs.

The tactical officer was screaming for the ship to get underway and I advised her there was no way to do that. It was clear to me what needed to be done, but not my place to suggest it until asked. Had the *Bolster* had their own master diver, he would've been the one to deliver the bad news to the captain.

The captain looked down on me and asked what I thought needed to be done. I replied that she should disconnect from the submarine, then pull back into the pier. She asked why the tugs couldn't maneuver us both back into the pier and I told her there's a 90-foot chain dragging on the bottom that needed to be disconnected. "Send me down a scuba team and a three-inch line."

Two divers were dressed in record time and a ladder was put over the side for them to get down to the water. Once in the water, they swam over to the boat, which was now tied off. I gave them instructions to go down the hawser to the bottom and find the connection between the hawser and the chain and tie the three-inch line to that connection.

I then specifically warned them not to go anywhere near the port propeller as I didn't want the line to become fouled around the propeller. They left the surface and all the while the tactical officer was screaming for us to stop, but we didn't. The divers returned to the surface just five minutes later and told the ship's diving officer the job couldn't be done because the chain and line were moving all around on the bottom.

The diving officer aborted the dive and told the divers to come up the ladder. I said, "STOP!" I told both divers to get over here and once they were hanging on the side of the boat, I spoke quietly to them so no one else could hear me. "Here is your chance to be a fucking hero and one in which you are sure to get a medal. Get your ass back down there, wrap your legs around that chain, hang on tight, and tie the line to the chain. Do you understand me?"

"Roger that, Master Diver," they said, and despite the diving officer's objection, they both said, "Leaving the surface."

Both divers surfaced after a few minutes with a huge smile on their faces and looked at me and both said, "Job complete."

With that, they exited the water and I looked up at the captain and said, "Coming up on the line, ma'am," indicating that the three-inch line should be pulled up. The line was made fast to the ship's capstan and would bring the chain to the surface. The captain relayed the message to the ship's bos'n—the deck boss—to heave around on the capstan and the line started to come up. The moment it became taut, it led directly into the port screw. I screamed for them to stop, but it was too late and now it was fouled as well.

The captain, now emotionally drained, looked down and asked, "Where does it go, Master Diver?" I looked up and said, "Wait one minute, ma'am. Please don't move a thing."

I slid back into the dark waters of the Panama Canal and the last thing I heard was the tactical officer on the submarine shouting again for me to get out. I did my three slow breaths and left the surface pulling myself down, this time using the three-inch line. The line was now buried deep under the fourteen-inch hawser and was pulled tight.

I returned to the surface and asked the captain to slack the line. The moment it was done, I went back down to the port propeller again holding my breath. This time I lifted the line up and over a blade so both ends were coming out between the same two blades. Now nothing was preventing us from pulling up the chain except for the three-inch line being pinched under the fourteen-inch hawser. I returned to the surface and crawled back into the boat and said, "Coming up, ma'am."

The Captain yelled to her Bos'n to come up on the capstan and the three-inch line became taut again. When a three-inch line is about to snap, its diameter can decrease almost by half. The Bos'n stopped the capstan and said, "That's it, captain."

She peered over the side looking for support and asked, "Master Diver?"

I looked up at her and she looked as if she was ready to quit and I said, "Coming up, ma'am."

I heard her pass the message to the bos'n and he said he wouldn't do it because it wasn't' safe.

She again looked over the side. "Master Diver?"

I repeated, "Coming up, ma'am."

I heard the tone of her voice change as she spoke louder and now with authority. "Bos'n, you're relieved. On the capstan, coming up one (slowly)."

The moment the line started to move, it popped out from under the hawser, and the ship was able to recover the anchor chain and disconnect from the submarine.

I returned to *Salvor* and my captain greeted me on the fantail. I was soaking wet and he asked what happened to me? The other divers were snickering, but kept their mouths shut. I explained what had happened and what I did and told my captain that once the tactical officer in command could get off the submarine, he would be coming to see him. He just said for me to go get cleaned up and he would take care of him.

Once showered and in a fresh uniform, my presence was requested in the wardroom. My captain, the *Bolster*'s captain, and the tactical officer as well as our two executive officers were waiting on me. I went in expecting to get my ass chewed, but nothing was said about my actions and freediving under the ship. Instead, I was asked to assist in the repairs of both the *Bolster* and the damaged submarine. The *Bolster*'s diving officer said they could handle the wrapped-up hawser and the crushed rope guard, and if we could repair and re-rig the submarine, we could all leave the following day. I agreed and went to talk with my divers.

We took a scuba team over to the nose of the submarine to have a look at the damage below. The divers were not long before coming back and letting me know the nose cone itself was undamaged, but the 1 5/8" inch safety shackle was completely destroyed and was elongated. It would need to come off the nose cone before we could replace it with another one. However, the shackle was so bent that removing it by any conventional method was out of the question.

This type of problem was exactly why the U.S. Navy has master divers. The culmination of years of study and practical application formed an expertise to handle such circumstances. I looked at my chief and simply said, "Go onboard and get me the Kerie cable kit." Everyone's eyes went wide and all of them together repeated Kerie cable?

Kerie cable is not widely used and most Navy divers have never even seen it used. Kerie cable is nothing more than a flexible exothermic cutting torch that needs very little power to operate. Oxygen is force-fed through a plastic-coated steel cable. The only items needed are the cable itself, oxygen regulator, and a bottle of oxygen. Once lit off, the Kerie cable looks more like a roman candle, but it will cut virtually anything, in this case a hardened 1 5/8" inch damaged shackle. Of course, the operator needed to use extreme caution to avoid losing fingers or a hand.

The divers were in the water and the Kerie cable was set up on the front of the submarine. We were ready to go to work when both captains showed up on the pier to ask how things were going. I answered that the shackle was badly damaged and elongated and we needed to remove it.

The captains looked at one another and asked how I was going to do that. I looked behind me and said, "O2 (oxygen) on?"

The operator said, "Yes, Master Diver. I had a BIC lighter in my hand and lit the Kerie cable. Sparks flew six feet into the air as I passed it to the divers, and said to the captains, "Kerie cable."

They were both against using it as they knew very little about it, but before they were done protesting, the divers came up and said, "Job complete." I then asked the captain of the *Bolster* if she wanted the standard 1 5/8 inch safety shackle or to upgrade to a 2-inch shackle. My captain again told her to listen to me and use a larger shackle, but again she declined.

CHAPTER 13

MAN OVERBOARD

Both ships and submarines got underway the next day and this time our departure was uneventful. Even though I had qualified as an officer of the deck, I was no longer on the watch bill because the captain said he had enough junior officers to stand watch. However, the captain asked me to be the senior watch bill coordinator, a task usually assigned to a senior officer. In that role, I selected the officer of the deck for each time period.

I didn't mind standing watches on the bridge. In fact, I liked it so when I wrote the watch bill, I would take what we called the dog-watch each day from 1600 to 1800. I took this watch because it was only two hours and it gave everyone the chance to eat and I always wanted to eat last. That way, I could ensure that the cooks were doing a good job, because if there wasn't enough food for me, then it would be hell for them.

We were underway for only a few days after leaving Panama when one of the officers became ill. I asked her what watch she had and she said mid-watch (0000-0400).

I told her to stay in bed and I would be happy to take her watch. I went up to the bridge and the previous officer of the deck was surprised to see me. I told him I was filling in for his relief, who was sick. Before leaving, he told me the tactical officer in command had us steaming in series, which meant one ship and sub directly in front of the other set. I remarked at the stupidity in that logic as I assumed the watch.

The captain himself taught me how to stand officer of the deck and one of his pointers to me was when you take the watch at night take a white grease pencil and mark all the targets on the radar screen with an X. Although the quartermasters, who oversaw the bridge, hated seeing their radar screens marked up, it was a quick way to ensure the other ships stayed at a distance.

Just fifteen minutes into the watch, I walked up to the radar screen and immediately noticed that the submarine that *Bolster* was towing was no longer where I had placed an X. She was farther back and the gap was expanding. I called the *Bolster*'s bridge via the VHF Radio and asked if they were paying out wire and they said no. I then told them to check the tow and seconds later they radioed back they lost it.

The drifting submarine was coming straight toward us. When you are towing a submarine, you cannot turn quickly and even small course changes will cause the tow wire to hop across the water and shake the ship. I yelled: "Right five-degree rudder!" You could feel the shutter throughout the ship, but it had no effect on our course.

I then yelled: "Right ten-degree rudder!" But again it didn't change our course enough for us to miss the incoming submarine. Now the tow line was hopping out of the water and everyone onboard knew something was wrong.

Lastly, I yelled out: "Right fifteen-degree rudder!" The sound and vibration throughout the ship was now deafening. The captain, executive officer, and navigator ran up to the bridge. The captain shouted: "What the hell is going on?"

I pointed to our port side and the drifting submarine. He asked what I was doing on watch and I said the oncoming officer was sick so I took her watch. He replied, "Thank God it was you on watch!"

The following day *Bolster* recovered her tow and they discovered that the 1 5/8 inch safety shackle had broken. When the captain heard the news on the bridge, he just looked over at me and gave me a smile. It took the rest of the day for *Bolster* to reconnect the submarine and now it was towing on the secondary towing rig.

When ships or submarines are prepared for a tow two separate pendants are used. The secondary pendant or emergency pendant is rigged in a fashion that a ship can recover the tow in any sea condition. The secondary is rigged with a floating polypropylene line and a buoy which is tied down the length of the submarine and trails three hundred feet behind the tow. In the event the ship loses its primary pendant, it navigates behind the vessel and captures the buoy and brings the secondary pendant aboard. We slowed down for the day to allow them time to reclaim their tow.

It is impossible to stop whilst towing at sea because of the weight of the tow wire and chain. With 2000 feet of wire out and another 180 feet of chain connected to the submarine, the combined weight would simply pull the two vessels together causing a collision. The 3700 tons of submarine would cause catastrophic damage to our ship. So, while the *Bolster* was reclaiming its tow, we slowed down but kept our wire tight.

The *Salvor* was one of the first ships in the Pacific to get women permanently assigned onboard. In fact, it was the previous leadership's poor decision to fraternize with some of the women onboard that caused the captain and executive officer and several others to get relieved for cause. In doing so, the *Salvor's* reputation was soiled and the admiral was concerned and called me and the captain to his office prior to our next deployment. The admiral asked us what our plan was to ensure something like that would never happen again. My captain looked at me and said, "Explain it, Senior Chief."

We had a very bold plan which had never been instituted onboard any other Navy ship. I told the admiral that we wanted to start a zero-dating policy. He asked how that was going to work and I explained, no one will be allowed to date another sailor onboard and if they did, they would be subject to non-judicial punishment, a process reserved for minor, non-criminal offenses, and the senior sailor would be transferred off the ship. The punishment most common for such offenses is called 30/30: thirty days of restrictions and thirty days of extra duty, and a small amount of pay each month for up to ninety days. The maximum time a commanding officer can give is 90/90.

The admiral told us to go ahead and see how it worked. Before the meeting ended, I had one more suggestion. After noting that the ship with the senior officer present aboard flies a commandant pennant, I suggested making the Enlisted Surface Warfare Qualifications mandatory for all petty officers and above onboard. "When the command hits eighty percent of the crew, I want to fly a, Enlisted Surface warfare pennant." The qualifications involve learning all aspects of the ship, not just your job, but also damage control, engineering, weapon systems, navigation, and communications.

The admiral laughed and said, "Senior Chief, if you can do that, I will provide you with the pennant myself."

Several days later, the seas had calmed down and the tactical officer in command invited everyone available over to the escort combat vessel for a barbeque and volleyball match. About fifty sailors each from *Salvor* and *Bolster* would take part, while the rest of the crews would stay aboard to safely operate the ship.

The escort vessel was tasked with transportation for the event since their boats were larger, but it still took several runs to get the crew over to the destroyer. It was a beautiful day with calm seas and a blue sky, and everyone was enjoying themselves while the cooks barbequed a feast. Although there was quite a bit of rivalry between the ships during the volleyball match, it was all in good fun and it was a nice afternoon to just unwind and relax.

I sat with the command master chief of the escort vessel swapping sea stories and he told me there were 330 sailors in his crew. That impressed me since it was three times the crew onboard the *Salvor*.

"Yeah, three times the number of headaches," he replied. He said that every week a sailor was sent to captain's mast and that seemed to be consuming all his time onboard. The biggest difference between civilian law and Non-Judicial Punishment is that in civilian law the burden is on the court to prove you are guilty. In the military, no such rule exists and the commanding officer only needs to believe you are guilty.

When I told the command master chief we hadn't had a Non-Judicial Punishment in over six months, he looked at me and said, "Well then, Senior Chief, you and your captain must be doing things right." He thought the influence of women in the crew played a role. He said women have a calming influence over men, which minimizes hormones associated with aggressive behavior.

I agreed, as I never saw a fist fight while I was on board the ship. I told him we had a no dating policy as well that was not only working, but it also allowed the crew to relax around one another without worrying if the other would have an ulterior motive. He looked skeptical and I said, "I'm not so naïve as to think it isn't happening, but if it is, I have no knowledge of it, and that means the sailors are being totally discrete. And that's good enough for me."

The afternoon was finally coming to an end onboard our escort ship and I waited until the last boat to ensure everyone got home safely. Our escort ship had a few female officers onboard and one young ensign was the boat officer for that last ride back. On small boats, typically four sailors are assigned for its safe operation, boat officer, coxswain, engineer, and a deck seaman (also called a bow hook).

The swells started to pick up, but it wasn't rough. Senior sailors board small boats last and to the rear. I climbed in, then we were off. The young ensign decided to go to *Bolster* first to drop off their remaining sailors. Now the swells were getting larger as they normally do late in the afternoon and the coxswain attempted to come alongside the *Bolster*, which was moving at twelve knots. Sitting in the back of the boat, I sensed something was wrong and the advice the master chief gave me long ago was singing out loud in my head. *If it don't feel right, it ain't right.*

As the boat got closer, the ensign moved and was now standing on the port side between the ship and the boat's cabin. I yelled out to her: "Don't stand there!" But she just froze and it looked as if the ship was going to smash her up against the cabin. So, I bolted forward grabbing her by the life jacket and threw her toward the bow of the boat and in doing so the ship impacted me instead.

My ship's bos'n (Ed) grabbed me and asked if I was okay. I said yes, but I felt a small stitch in my side. We returned to the *Salvor* and I went below to change and now the stitch was making it difficult to breathe. The bos'n told the captain what had happened and when he came to check on me, he took one look and sent me to medical. The official diagnosis was separated ribs; the muscle separated from bone on two ribs when the *Bolster* impacted me.

A week later, the weather turned rough, but the crew and I had been at sea for weeks so we were all doing our best to cope with it. Underway you are constantly training should a real emergency occur. Damage control and firefighting is at the top of the list and we do so much of it that it becomes monotonous. However, while towing, one of the drills that cannot be done is man overboard since our steering is restricted. When the weather is rough, the outer decks are secured and the only way to access them is with the captain's permission.

I stopped what I was doing when I heard my name called out over the 1MC, the ship's microphone. "Master Diver Bettua, your presence is requested on the bridge."

The higher you go on a ship at sea, the more roll you feel and the bridge seems to move much more than the main deck. As I reached the bridge, I needed to hang onto something to steady myself. I could see *Bolster* out front with her tow and our escort vessel off in the distance on our starboard side, and white caps everywhere on the ocean.

The captain explained that an important electronic gadget was malfunctioning and that we needed to get parts off the escort vessel. He asked if I would drive the Rigid Inflatable Boat over to pick it up. "Nice day, captain," I responded, hoping he would put off the request until the seas calmed. But he insisted that the engineers really needed the part.

"Roger that!"

He then asked if I would mind taking a young engineer with me, exclaiming each week since we left Hawaii this petty officer would put a note in the captain's suggestion box asking to go for a ride in the Rigid Inflatable Boat with the master diver. Also going with me would be the electronics chief. Normally I only operated the lifeboat with my divers, who were all in great shape, fantastic swimmers, and stayed calm in any situation. But now my team was an overzealous engineer looking for a thrill ride and a scared chief petty officer who couldn't swim.

A towed submarine never follows in a straight line. It normally will hang off the port or starboard side. The worst-case scenario is when the submarine "hunts" which means it goes from the extreme left to the extreme right back and forth. This 637-class submarine was trailing about fifty yards off of our port side, the same side where we launch and return the lifeboat.

The distance between the rear of the ship and where the tow wire enters the water is about 100 feet astern. Then there's another 1700 feet of wire which goes underwater coupled to 180 feet of chain. It's the weight of the two, which form a catenary, that is approximately 150 feet deep, and this creates a giant shock absorber. During any evolution on the fantail, like launching the lifeboat, the wire is captured by two massive hydraulic pins. This prevents the wire from sweeping toward sailors and possibly injuring or killing them. My divers would operate the davit—a small crane for lowering the craft—and also all the positions on the fantail, two divers on the aft line and two or three more on the forward line, also called the sea painter. My two passengers and I had life jackets and hardhats on and we were ready to go. The ship's bos'n, a warrant officer and a good friend named Ed, was in charge of the evolution.

It is always very unnerving launching a boat and as you look behind you see a 2 1/8 inch wire cutting through the ocean. What would make matters worse today was the swells were ten feet or better. I had the electronics chief in the rear of the boat on the deck and the engineer in the bow. He would disconnect the sea painter line the moment I was ready to pull away. The sea painter line is crucial in keeping the bow of the boat next to the ship and the nose pointed up seas. Without such a line the bow of the lifeboat could fall away from the ship turning sideways to the seas and possibly flipping over.

I told my passengers to hold on tight as we went up and over the rail. I started the boat before it hit the water. The impact sent them both to the deck and I quickly unhooked from the davit. The aft line was thrown over and I moved the boat forward slightly to create slack on the sea painter. He disconnected it and we pulled out in a wide arc and watched the sub get closer before finally passing us on our starboard side.

I looked at the submarine as it went by since I needed to inspect the tow every few days. Finally, the secondary line and buoy went by as well. We didn't need to navigate up to the destroyer, because she came back to us and turned beam to the seas. All 535 feet blocked the incoming waves and now the ocean was nothing more than a lake. I pulled up to the crane and a hook was waiting to lift us onboard.

As the boat came up to the main deck, the command master chief was waiting for me and greeted me with a laugh by saying, "You couldn't pick a better day?"

I laughed along with him and said, "Well, I don't get to pick the day." The engineer and electronics chief were escorted to the engineering department and the command master chief asked me to follow him. "The ship's conning officer wants to meet you." The conning officer is second in command of the bridge under the Officer of the Deck and is responsible for the safe navigation of the ship.

He walked me up to the bridge and once I stepped in, I was amazed at not only its sheer size, but the amount of electronics onboard. I could see the *Salvor* off in the distance and it was dwarfed by comparison to this ship.

Then a familiar face walked up to me, the ensign who was the boat officer. She said, "Senior Chief, I want to thank you for looking after me last week, and I'm sorry you got hurt." I went to shake her hand, but she wrapped her arms around me like she was hugging her favorite uncle and squeezed tight enough for me to writhe in pain from my hurt ribs.

As the command master chief and I walked off the bridge, he snickered and said, "I sure hope that little girl didn't hurt you, Master Diver." We laughed all the way down to the chief's mess.

After a very satisfying lunch, it was time to go home and the ship's captain met us at the lifeboat. He just wanted to meet me and asked where I would like to get dropped.

I explained the perfect spot would be forward of the *Salvor* on the port side. That way I could just drift back to her and would not have to go head on into the seas. He said that was no problem. I used my portable VHF Radio to call over to *Salvor* and explain where the destroyer was planning on putting us in.

Minutes later you could hear the gas turbine engines spinning up and the ship leaped forward at thirty knots to get ahead of and cross *Salvors* bow. The process took only minutes and the ship was now stopped and was maneuvering to come beam to the seas. We were in the boat and lowered down in an instant, then pulled away from the ship.

The Destroyer once again leaped forward and crossed ahead of *Salvor* and took station off her starboard side. Being in a small boat in large seas can be daunting, but the Navy didn't skimp on inferior products. Our ship's lifeboat was the very best rigid inflatable boat money could buy, built for commercial and military use. It had a unique system that would allow water to go inside the hull when the boat was at rest or a slow idle. This provided a lower center of gravity and it was near impossible to flip at low speeds.

As we waited for *Salvor* to get closer, I briefed the two passengers. I had the young, excited engineer in the front of the boat and told him the most important thing for him to do was to attach the sea painter line when I told him. That is the only line we really needed and without it, we would get in trouble. The electronics chief was in the rear of the boat and scared to death, so I just said, "Chief, just hold on when I start to go along side."

Now the ship was close and I turned the boat up sea so I could match the *Salvors* speed. As we moved along with the ship, I watched the wire cut through the water and waited for the signal from Ed to move in. The ship bos'n motioned for us to come alongside and I yelled to my passengers. "Hold on! Here we go!"

Moving alongside a ship in heavy seas is twice as difficult as navigating through the sea without the ship. Waves hit the side of the ship and come back toward you which causes a washing machine effect. The lifeboat came in perfectly and I yelled for the engineer to connect the sea painter and he did. Then I ordered the passengers to get down on the deck and then snapped the davit hook into the lifeboat lifting sling.

At this point, there was nothing left for me to do apart from shutting off the engine. Before the bos'n could pull up the lifeboat, the sea painter line came off and now the nose was pulling away from the ship.

The boat was now being dragged through the seas sideways and water filled the forward area of the boat causing it to dip even lower into the sea and the next wave mercilessly slammed into the sunken bow, and jackknifed the lifeboat, catapulting the engineer overboard. As he went over, I grabbed his life jacket with my left hand and the steering wheel with my other hand. In doing so the force was so great, I bent the steering wheel hard over to the port side. I was in an awkward position, and the next wave washed me out.

Both the captain and the executive officer were in the wardroom and heard something no captain ever wants to hear over the 1MC. "Man overboard, man overboard, port side. I say again, man overboard, man overboard, port side."

What made matters worse was that the submarine was bearing down on the port side. We both were now violently tumbling in the ship's wash caused by the propellers, one arm covering my head and the other latched onto the back of the engineer's life vest. As soon as I could get my head above the water, I was looking for that wire, while still holding onto the engineer's life jacket. I saw the wire coming toward us and screamed for the engineer to kick. Not letting go of his life jacket at the back of his neck I swam as hard as I could whilst pulling him. Something very un-natural about being in your ship's propeller wash while watching her steam away!

The wire just narrowly missed us, but the submarine was still coming. I screamed over and over again for the engineer to just kick while I used a modified side stroke to pull us out past the incoming submarine and when it went by at 12 knots, we were close enough to touch her. Now the captain was on the bridge and with his binoculars he watched in horror as I struggled to get past the submarine, and he didn't know if we made it or not until the submarine passed us.

The executive officer ran to the fantail to see if he could help. But by this time the destroyer had been notified that *Salvor* had a man overboard and she was coming to save the day. As she broke away from her standard formation, I saw her rooster tail and she was coming at top speed which was over forty knots. The *Salvor* had now pulled the swamped lifeboat from the sea with the electronics chief still onboard, hanging on like an Alabama tick. Once it was on the deck, my divers prepared to come get us. But it would take several of them to bend the steering wheel back into place before they could drive the boat.

Now still holding onto the engineer's life jacket after the submarine passed, I realized that I could hear the bridges of the two ships coordinating our rescue. That was because when I was thrown out of the lifeboat, my knife somehow caught the portable VHF radio lanyard, which miraculously was floating behind my head. I grabbed it and radioed all stations and let them know we were okay. The destroyer pulled up seconds later to provide a lee for shelter and our lifeboat arrived and pulled us to safety.

CHAPTER 14

NOT TODAY MASTER CHIEF

Two years later, in early 1995 the *Salvor* was awarded the "Marjorie Sterrett Battleship Award" for being the most battle-ready ship in the Pacific fleet. That's how long it took to transform a ship from one with a salacious past to one with a stellar reputation. *Salvor* was also the only ship in Pearl Harbor flying the Enlisted Surface Warfare Specialist (ESWS) pennant on its mast. The presence of the pennant meant extra work for the crew, and it didn't make everyone onboard happy.

Being a good leader does not necessarily mean winning popularity contests with the crew. The mandatory ESWS program onboard was highly controversial and several petty officers and even a few chiefs didn't appreciate the fact I was holding their evaluations at bay until they were completed. The disgruntled chiefs requested an audience with the squadron command master chief to complain about the mandatory program. But their ramblings fell on deaf ears and the master chief said he agreed whole heartedly with the program and wished more ships in the harbor would follow suit.

We must have done a good job towing that 637-class submarine from Panama to Bremerton, Washington because we got the very same mission again. However, this time I had a very seasoned crew, one that felt more like a big family. Everyone onboard knew their job and it was my job to listen to their needs and see if I could make life aboard better for everyone.

One issue was access to the ship's weight room and gym. Only a few people were allowed to use it at a time, and it was only available during certain hours. I discussed the problem with the captain and suggested we put the crew on flex hours. That meant the crew could work out any time of day as long as they weren't on watch. As a result, crew members could utilize the facility twenty-four hours a day.

The crew's favorite pastime while underway was karaoke on the mess decks and everyone joined in, even the captain and I, and it was hilarious. The night before pulling into San Diego, I asked the crew if there was anything they wanted to do besides going down to Tijuana during our stay. Surprisingly, they asked if they could go to Disneyland. As the ship's morale, welfare, and recreation officer, I knew we had plenty of money to support the event. I looked at the captain and he nodded in agreement. I yelled out, "We're going to Disneyland."

I put a sign-up sheet on our bulletin board and to my surprise seventy-two sailors wanted to go. The rest of the crew would have to stay aboard to ensure the ship was safe. I rented four new 18-passenger vans and packed each one with our crew, and off we went. Disneyland was about two hours away from San Diego and I made sure there would be no side excursions by putting either an officer or chief in each van. Paying for seventy-two Disneyland tickets and four vans would cost the *Salvor* over $10,000, but it was money well spent. Everyone had a great time!

Sailors being sailors they asked if they could drink on the ride back to the ship in the vans. I said no problem as long as the driver and co-pilot in the front seats didn't drink and that everyone behaved. They gave me their word they would look out for one another during the ride. We got back to the base about 2300 and I was the co-pilot of the first van.

I introduced myself as the command senior chief and told the guards the four vans were on a ship's function. The senior guard responded by saying: "Well, I don't believe you are on a ship's function and I certainly don't believe you are a senior chief."

Granted, I was a very young senior chief, but I went from happy-go-lucky just spent the day at Disney Land, to vicious, in a fraction of a second, and bounced my ID card off the guard's nose!

He looked at it, apologized and said, "Please carry on."

When we got back to the ship, the command duty officer met me on the quarterdeck and asked what happened because the base security called and said there was an altercation at the front gate. I just said that a gate guard was being rude and went below to go to sleep.

Resting in my rack the next morning at 0630, I heard my name called. "Senior Chief Bettua, lay to the captain's cabin." It was the first time that I'd ever been called on the ship's 1MC without the speaker adding: "Your presence is requested." It was a sign of respect and for them not to use it meant I was possibly in trouble. Lay to, is a term to move quickly from a senior to a subordinate.

I jumped up and threw my uniform on and bolted up the three flights of stairs. All I could think of was someone was making an issue of me dressing down the gate guard. I entered the captain's (Randy) stateroom and saw that he was holding a "Navy Blue," which meant it was correspondence from an admiral or above. The executive officer (John), who is the second in command, was there as well.

The executive officer had his hands on his head mumbling, "I can't believe we are going to lose you." Then the captain asked what happened last night. I explained the gate guards were disrespectful and questioned my rank when we were coming onto the base. The captain just shook his head and said let me make sure I got this right, what is your Social Security number, Senior Chief? I told him and asked what was this all about.

He smiled and said the Chief of Naval Operations, a four-star admiral wanted to congratulate and welcome me as the youngest master chief petty officer of the Navy at age thirty-three. They shouted together: "Master Chief!" I had no idea I was even eligible. In fact, I thought I needed to wait another year. But because of my performance I was selected early.

"Go ahead and get cleaned up. I am frocking you to master chief today," the captain said.

I remember leaving his cabin in a bit of a fog thinking to myself, *I hope this isn't some sort of a mistake or joke like the master diver had played on me in Israel.* So, on my way back down to my berthing compartment, I knocked on the radio department's secure door. I knew if a Navy blue came into the ship, they would have been the ones to print it and hand deliver it to the captain. My chief radioman answered the door, smiled and said: "Congratulations, Master Chief."

Our transit down to Panama was over before we knew it. As we steamed into the entrance of the canal, new orders directed us to go through the Panama Canal and pick up our tow on the Atlantic side. I have to admit the last few weeks of being a master chief had brought about more spring in my step and a constant smile on my face.

All those years working for master chief/master divers had paid off and now I was one as well. During our transit through the canal, I marveled on how it was built, especially since it was constructed in 1904. For 23 years, the Panamanians attempted to complete the canal linking the Pacific to the Atlantic but were unsuccessful.

American engineers completed the job in just ten years from 1904-1914. The canal is only 180 feet wide and 51 miles long, which includes several lakes and takes about six hours to transit. The Pacific side is eight inches higher than the Atlantic side, therefore several locks are used to safely pass. We met our Atlantic counterpart and our tow near the town of Cristobal on a very stormy night.

The following day the rain finally stopped and my divers and I went over to check the tow. We needed to examine the primary and secondary tow pennants, the anchor and the alarm and lighting system. The alarm system was crucial onboard a submarine as it was the only means of informing our ship if the submarine was taking on water. The system consisted of an operating panel, light mast, and float switches inside the submarine.

If a float switch was actuated, it would turn on a light on the mast to inform us on the ship. We would need to go below decks on the sub and physically look at each float switch throughout the ship. There were low-level float switches and high-level float switches, which would trigger either a yellow light (low level) or a red light (high level) on the mast. This inspection would need to be done with flashlights since no power existed onboard. Once I was satisfied with the condition of the sub, we returned to the ship and were ready to get underway.

The transit speed through the canal was eight knots and a Panamanian pilot was in charge of the bridge while the submarine was at "short stay." Short stay is a very dangerous period when the tow wire has very little or no catenary and it is that catenary that provides a shock absorber between the towing vessel and sub. My job was on the fantail and I would pay out or recover the tow wire accordingly depending on the tension to keep the tow wire in the water.

Once through the locks we wasted no time leaving the Panamanian pilot behind and heading out to sea. As the ship moved into deeper water, my job was to pay out the tow wire in small increments until it reached 1800 to 2000 feet. Then I adjusted the length to ensure the submarine was in step with the same rhythm as our ship before finally securing it for the day.

Several days passed at sea and now the weather was rough and everyone was doing their best to cope with the conditions. That's when the officer of the deck informed me the submarine had an intermittent yellow light. I walked up to the bridge clinging to anything that wasn't moving and I found the captain, who was peering through binoculars at the mast on the tow. He looked at me and said, "Intermittent yellow master chief."

We talked it over and agreed to wait. It could just be a small amount of water moving back and forth triggering the lower float alarm. Besides the ocean was very rough and it would be no walk in the park getting onboard her.

I went back down below to the dive locker and told my chief to make sure the Rigid Inflatable Boat was ready to go. I also told him to choose four of the most competent divers and tell them to be ready to go with life jackets, hardhats, flashlights, and harnesses to snap into the submarine safety rail. All submarines have a track that runs the length of the sub which is built into the deck. This railing is for safety purposes and submariners snap into it when the sub is on the surface in rough weather.

Later that afternoon the light went to steady yellow, and then red, ten minutes later. It was time for action. I asked the captain if we could slow down to eight knots and quarter the seas to protect the boat during the launch and he agreed. Quartering the seas meant changing the direction of the ship by 15-20 degrees from head-on to the waves to create slightly less wave action for the boat.

When I briefed my men, I emphasized the importance of the sea painter to keep the lifeboat from turning sideways to the waves, getting pummeled and flipping over. I didn't want another man-overboard incident. They all smiled and said, "Roger that, Master Chief."

I couldn't have asked for a better team and two of them later in their career would become master divers. The chief would drive and four of us would go aboard the sub so we could check the alarm panel and locate the float senser causing the alarm. Then we would make our way to that sensor.

The ships Bos'n handled the launching and before we knew it waves were smashing our faces. The chief stayed focused and broke away from the ship as quickly as possible, and once away, we were going down sea, toward the sub. As we came up to it, we saw the sub's anchor, which was rigged aft, had come loose, and needed additional support. I told one of my divers to grab some line and when we were done inside, we would move back to the anchor and tie it off better.

The boat now maneuvered around to the starboard side taking cover behind the conning tower as the waves were washing over the top of the submarine. When the boat touched the sub, the four of us clambered up the ladder in seconds. We accessed the dark stale submarine and closed the hatch behind us.

It was pitch dark and quiet inside. Using flashlights, we found the alarm panel and saw that the sensor that was triggered was in the engine room at the rear of the sub. To get there, we had to penetrate two watertight doors. I left a diver at each one as we moved farther into the sub. When I entered the engine room with one other diver, our flashlights cut through the pitch-black stale air. We found the bracket that was holding the sensors had broken off and was lying in the bilge.

The diver with me had the sense to bring along some heavy-duty tie wraps and he was able to secure the bracket and sensors so they were upright on the wall. We made our way back and at each hatch we secured the watertight doors. When we reached the alarm panel, we saw that no alarms were going off now.

Before going out on the weather deck, I told everyone that we would immediately snap into the rail before heading aft to the anchor. Once we were out and snapped in, we closed the hatch and secured it. The sun had set and it was getting darker by the minute. Waves were breaking over the deck and hitting our legs as we moved through the dusk. The closer we got to the back of the submarine, the larger the waves.

We were about twenty-five feet from the anchor when I saw the railing was damaged. We would have to unhook and then re-hook as quickly as possible on the other side of the broken railing. I told my divers to hang onto one another. I went first, then the others followed. Once at the anchor, we repositioned it and tied it off with the line we brought aboard. Waves were crashing all around us, and we were hanging onto the anchor for stability.

"Job complete," I shouted, and we moved forward.

The first diver came to the damaged rail and waited for the waves to pass, then transitioned perfectly. He held onto the next diver and pulled him forward so he could snap in again. The second diver did the same for the third diver. Then it was my turn.

The moment I disconnected, one of the others yelled: "Watch out!"

I looked up just in time to see a freak wave blast completely over the top of the submarine. It struck me in the chest, I lost my grip, and in a flash, I was flying overboard. It all felt like slow motion and in my mind, I knew there was a high likelihood that it would be too dark to find me.

At the very moment I thought I was gone, a huge arm punched through the wave and grabbed me. A young diver named Todd Corley said, "Not today, Master Chief!"

He snapped me back into the rail. I felt blessed and grateful that I'd survived. We all moved forward and exited the submarine.

A few months later, we were back in Pearl Harbor and one night, about 10 p.m., I received a phone call from my ship's command duty officer. He said my presence was requested at Tripler Army Hospital. I asked why and he said he only knew that they requested the command master chief. In fact, it was my job to handle cases where sailors were hospitalized. I got dressed and drove to the hospital only to find an empty emergency room.

After reporting to the desk, a doctor and a chaplain walked out to see me. They asked if Petty Officer Corley worked for me, and I said he did. The doctor's next words caught me off guard. He said Todd Corley had been in an accident and would pass away soon. "Would you like to be there with him?"

"Yes, of course."

The doctor warned me that he had major trauma damage to his head and asked if I would be okay. I replied yes but didn't know what I was about to see. As he led me into his room, there was no way anyone could be prepared. Here was one of my closest shipmates who had saved my life and was about to expire. I held his hand and tried not to focus on the trauma while I watched and listened to the EKG machine.

Gradually, the beeps slowed. Tears were flowing out of my eyes and finally, Todd flatlined. It was the hardest thing to witness, but I was glad I was there to hold his hand to the very end.

As I walked out to the waiting room to compose myself, the captain, XO, and their wives rushed through the doors together. Still wearing dinner dress uniforms and gowns, they had come directly from a formal function. I gave them the bad news that Todd was gone. Todd's wife was also involved in the accident and they were taking care of her injuries in another room when all of us walked in to give her the news. Of course, she was distraught and everyone in the room was crying. None of us wanted to believe it had happened.

Then the captain said he would talk to the casualty assistance control officers and find a good one to assist her in getting them both back to Todd's home state. The moment that was suggested, Todd's wife erupted, "No fucking way, I want Master Chief Bettua to bring Todd home. Everyone looked at me and the captain said, "Master Chief, will you do it?"

Of course, I said.

Casualty assistance control officers were trained and assigned for such reasons and it was not normal for a command master chief to take on that responsibility. This series of tasks would start in Hawaii with getting the wife's household goods completely packed out and shipped. Then I was to accompany Todd and his wife to Wisconsin and coordinate a full military burial.

Bringing a shipmate home to his parents is one of the most difficult things I have ever had to do. Once there, the family tasked me with picking out and designing Todd's headstone. I chose a black marble with a deep-sea diver engraved on it. I knew he would've loved it. The second task was a bit more difficult and it was to give Todd's eulogy in front of the entire town.

The Navy had also sent the regional officer from Chicago to oversee the military burial. I asked her for two American flags to drape on top of Todd's casket. She said no, and that became a big deal. I told her I was not giving a flag to the wife without giving one to his mother, but the commander continued to resist. Finally, I told her to get a second flag, or I will have one flown from Pearl Harbor via express mail. One way or another, I insisted we would have two flags on that casket, and finally she conceded.

The town's priest came and spoke to me about what he expected in Todd's eulogy. He said Todd was a football star in high school, but no one knew what he did in the Navy or how he died. I told the priest I would talk about how Todd lived, not how he died. During the eulogy, I explained what it meant to be a Navy deep sea diver and also how Todd had saved my life.

This experience was fraught with emotions: sadness, grief, but also pride. I was honored to bring Todd home to his family. He was my friend and a great shipmate.

CHAPTER 15

SEMPER FI

The Navy was having difficulties finding a master diver willing to go work with Marine Corps Force Reconnaissance units. The job description specified the master diver needed to be young and physically fit in order to keep up. I volunteered for the job because no one else wanted it, but for some reason I needed to be vetted first by the command master chief of the Bureau of Naval Personnel

Although we were both the same rank, it was clear on the phone call he was much older than I was, and he also had a position of authority. So, I addressed him as sir. He didn't like that much and said, "Listen to me, hot shot, if you think you can keep up with these marines, pack your bags and head to Camp LeJeune, North Carolina".

My orders were for me to report to the base's commanding officer who was a one-star brigadier general. Prior to reporting for duty one of the things I did was study the Marine Corps rank structure so I didn't embarrass myself. I was directed to the headquarters building and after parking, I saw a red flag with a single star out front of the building. As I walked up the steps a marine was walking down and I could see from his collar device he was a sergeant major. But before I could greet him, he said, "Morning Chief."

I figured if this sergeant major was not going to recognize my rank and demote me by two ranks, I would do the same to him. I replied, "Good morning, Gunny."

He shouted out, "Woah, woah, woah, that's Sergeant Major." I looked at him and said, "And I'm a master chief!" He then asked me to sit down on the steps with him where he explained that he thought all chiefs in the Navy responded to chief.

I asked him where he learned that and he said he called all the corpsman (medics) chiefs, and they didn't seem to mind.

"Well sergeant major, I'm no corpsman. I'm a Navy master diver." He shook my hand and said, "Well, I stand corrected. Thank you, Master Chief for squaring me away."

I walked into the massive building and followed the signs to the general's office and was greeted immediately by the general. He invited me in and asked if I would like a cup of coffee. We made small talk while we waited for the base's sergeant major to arrive. I heard footsteps approaching and the very same marine I spoke to on the steps walked in and we both laughed. The general asked if we knew one another and the sergeant major smiled and said we did.

We all sat down for a talk and the general said they had been waiting a year for the Navy to fill this assignment. I told him I didn't know it was that long, but I was specially screened because of my age and physical fitness.

The general responded: "Well, you certainly look fit, but there's no way you look like you could be an E-9. The sergeant major said that he'd already made that mistake. The gist of the conversation was that Force Recon and Recon were the black sheep of the Marine Corps and were a very rowdy bunch, who would test my resolve.

I asked how so and the sergeant major explained that I would be the most senior enlisted person at the command, and that they only have a first sergeant (E-8) in charge.

"Let me give you a piece of advice," the general added. "If you take shit from anyone junior to you, then you deserve it. Understand?"

"Yes, General."

"Lastly, although I am attaching you to Force Recon, you work directly for me and I will always have your back as long as you are right."

"I think he will do just fine," the sergeant major said.

The following morning, I joined Recon and Force Recon at 0630 for physical training. Navy divers typically wear black running shorts and a navy-blue t-shirt when working out. In my case, the t-shirt had a master diver logo on the back. The Marines wore black shorts and dark green t-shirts with their reconnaissance logo. I didn't think much about it and especially not that anyone would ever make an issue of it.

After the training, the commanding officer and executive officer invited me to discuss my duties and what they expected of me. It was quite a bit different being with the Marines and everything felt foreign. They used acronyms for everything and I had no idea what they were talking about. But once they saw my puzzled face, they would explain them to me. The commanding officer who was a colonel walked me around and introduced me to the administration staff and a young recon marine asked who I was. The colonel explained that I was a master diver and the young man shouted, "You're the new swim coach."

After we all laughed, the colonel said my new handle was "Coach", and that it was a good one. I agreed with him. Then the company gunnery sergeant stopped me to inform me I was out of uniform during morning physical training and that I needed to remedy that by the following morning. He said I should wear the same as everyone else, a green t-shirt with the reconnaissance logo on it.

In the Navy one thing we never do is wear an insignia that we didn't earn. The gunny didn't say it jokingly, and I couldn't believe an E-7 gunnery sergeant would be so brazen as to attempt to chastise an E-9. I could see the CO's eyes glanced at me to see what my response was going to be.

I calmly looked at the gunny and said, "What office is yours, Gunny. I'll come talk with you as soon as I'm done." He told me it was the last door on the right and walked down the hall. The colonel and the executive officer looked at me and the executive office said, "Master Chief, would you like me to take care of that?" I replied that I would handle it, that it needed to come from me.

I walked down the hall and entered the company gunnery sergeant's office, then shut and locked the door. Before he could get up from his chair behind his huge wooden desk, I shoved that desk and him all the way up against the back wall. He was half sitting and half standing with his arms locked down at his sides as he screamed like a little girl.

I leaned over, squeezed him tighter against the wall, and told him that I was an E-9 in United States Navy. "If you ever speak to me like that again, I'll make you wish you hadn't." I unlocked the door and walked out to find the hallway was filled with marines listening in on the conversation. Behind me, the gunny was still screaming. I walked past everyone and at the end of the hall the colonel and the major had big smirks on their faces. The colonel said, "Have a nice day, Coach."

The following day for physical training, I wore a dark green t-shirt with a black master diver emblem on the back.

The dive locker sat adjacent to the parachute loft and the marines who worked there were constantly teasing me about when I was going to make my first jump. Several of them were tandem-qualified and now bets were being made as to whether or not I had the nerve to jump out at 16,000 feet. That was the highest altitude one could jump out without using oxygen.

With over one hundred and twenty closed circuit Drager diving rigs and six transportable recompression chambers, I was busy getting all the equipment certified for use. But the barrage of teasing and bets continued until finally I said I would do it. The CO heard about it and asked if I really wanted to do it. I knew it was the only way to get them off my back, so I said I did.

A C130 aircraft was scheduled for the jump on Thursday and at least thirty free-fall jumpers were tagging along to see if I would chicken out and cancel the jump. It was a big week for us as we were trying to get ready for the commandant of the Marine Corps, a four-star general, coming to visit. The commandant was visiting Camp Lejeune and on his list of places to visit was the dive locker to meet his only master diver and talk about future diving in the Marine Corps.

On the morning of the jump, I wore a special Kevlar jumpsuit to protect me if we went into the bushes or trees. The most senior jumper, who would jump tandem with me, was a gunnery sergeant. I thought he might be a parachute packer, because he looked out of shape. I knew he couldn't be a recon marine.

The CO and XO met us all on the runway and again checked with me to ensure I was comfortable making the jump. I just said, "Let's get it done." I had work to do to get ready for my meeting with the commandant the next morning. They said they would meet me at the jump site after I landed.

The big C130 aircraft took off and during the entire flight everyone was doing their best to frighten me, but I just drowned them out. Finally at 16,000 feet, the back gate of the plane came open. We walked back, and I was amazed at how high we were. It was as if Earth was just a grey ball with the plane going 130 kts above it. The jump master spun me around so my back was to the rear of the plane and did his final checks. The last thing he said was. "Are you sure, Master Chief?"

I proudly shot two fingers up, and said, "Fuck you!" He shoved me in my chest with two hands and I flew out the back of the plane inverted. There was nothing fun about this jump. We tumbled several thousand feet before the other jumpers would finally get us under control. Once under control and my hands out to my side I could not wait for it to be over.

The chute opened and everything was going fine until the point where we were supposed to be slowing down. We didn't, and we hit the ground hard with my overweight tandem companion landing on top of me.

Holy shit that hurt! Both ankles and both knees were injured. The pain was so intense that I thought I was going to vomit. Now the CO and XO were on the scene as well as two independent duty corpsman who each shot me up with a dose of morphine and told me to hang on. US Navy's Independent Duty Corpsmen are some of the best trained medics you will ever find and during my career would render me aid many times. I don't remember the ambulance ride or the surgery, but when I woke up in my room the colonel and major as well as the two corpsmen were there.

I asked what happened and the colonel said it was a hard landing, and the gunny landed on top of me. He seemed really worried, but I assured him I would be fine. He told me he was worried the commandant would find no amusement in him allowing me to freefall and he thought he would get relieved of command. I said it was my fault and came up with a plan.

I told the two corpsmen to come and get me dressed and out of the hospital by 10 am. I said they should put me in the recompression chamber room, with a chair and my crutches. When the commandant comes in, he will see the crutches and tell me to sit when I attempt to stand. When he asks what happened, I will say I fell down, because that is the truth. The staged event went over perfectly and after our talk, the commandant told me to be more careful. "We can't afford you getting hurt." Then he departed.

As soon as his vehicle pulled away, the corpsmen took me back to the hospital. It would take a few months to recover from the jump, but it also earned me much respect with all the marines and especially the colonel.

Marines would come and go in the dive locker and at one point I thought the command was using it as a holding cell for the injured. The problem was that it took a fair amount of time to train the marines and get them qualified to work in the dive locker. Every now and then I needed more help and decided to interview a few marines for the position.

One marine in particular who carried himself well and was well spoken, impressed me enough to get the job. The sergeant (Shawn) was a huge man without an ounce of fat on him. He seemed pretty well reserved, and I thought he would make a good trainer for the other marines. The sergeant also had a natural ability to understand basic mechanics, and unlike many of the other shooters, he could actually turn a wrench.

Drager training was scheduled for the following week at the pool. It's a closed-circuit oxygen rebreather built for shallow water reconnaissance work. It's bubbleless when operated, so divers can't be detected by their bubbles. My men would be getting at least sixty Drager dive units ready to go.

The day came for us to train at the pool, which was a deep, twenty-five-yard-long training pool. For what we were doing, it was perfect. It had an average depth of twelve feet and could accommodate at least thirty divers at one time. Everyone was getting dressed and it was about time for me to do a briefing when I asked Shawn, the new sergeant, to move a few Drager containers. The look he gave me was something an E-9 would normally never see, especially not from a sergeant, who was a very junior E-5. I waved for him to come over and I could tell from his demeanor that he was very upset so I quietly asked him what was wrong? He wouldn't answer me so I said, "Sergeant, next time I ask you to do something just do it without all the attitude, please."

This absolutely enraged the sergeant, and he screamed at me, "That is it. I'm calling you out."

I was bewildered and had no idea of what he was talking about. That's when my staff sergeant (Mike), who was both well respected and well decorated, pushed through the crowd and stepped between us. He told the sergeant to stand down.

I'm sure my staff sergeant had received orders from the top to ensure my safety on the day I arrived. The young sergeant demanded it was his right to challenge me and for the staff sergeant to step aside. The staff sergeant told him that if he wanted a challenge, then he could challenge him.

The whole time I was trying to get clarification on what this challenge was all about. When I asked him, the staff sergeant explained that in Recon and Force Recon a junior marine can challenge a senior marine to a fight. I was just dumbfounded that something like this could occur in this day and age, but I remembered the general's advice and couldn't back down.

I asked my staff sergeant what the rules were and he said there were no rules other than I would get to choose the time and place. I said I choose right now in the deep end of the pool! The young sergeant ripped his shirt off like he was Hulk Hogan and yelled at me that he was going to kill me just prior to diving into the water. Now sixty marines were egging us both on, but the staff sergeant stood firm.

"Master Chief, I can't let you do this. He outweighs you by eighty pounds, and he's solid muscle."

I replied, "I know and that's what I'm counting on. I assured him I would be okay, but not to let either of us go too far and stop it if he thought it was unsafe. To my surprise, as I stripped off my shirt, all the marines were cheering me on. I guess everyone loves betting on the underdog.

I dove into the water, then started swimming out to the deep end of the pool where the massive sergeant was waiting for me. What he didn't know was I spent years being a lifeguard and my favorite pastime was spearfishing. I knew I could hold my breath longer than he could. I purposely got close to him when he was focused at cussing me out, I waited for that one big swing to come.

Right on cue, the sergeant threw a massive right hook and I ducked. As the swing went over my head, I shifted around, crawled up on his back and locked my arms tightly around his throat. As I hung on, I simply exhaled all the air out of my lungs and we both sank to the bottom of the pool. Between the both of us we had very little body fat and we hit the bottom of the pool with a thud.

Nothing on earth will humble a man quicker than not being able to breathe and being underwater makes it that much worse. My legs were wrapped around the sergeant's waist at the bottom of the pool, and I squeezed with my arms and my legs with everything I had.

The sergeant tapped out almost instantly, but I only wanted to do this challenge contest once so I kept him there maybe longer than necessary to teach him a lesson. As he started to lose consciousness and go limp, I swam him to the surface. A few marines jumped in to lend a hand getting the big sergeant to the side of the pool. He was spitting, sputtering, and coughing trying to catch his breath as he hung onto the side of the pool.

I climbed out of the water and asked if there was anyone else that felt the need to challenge me? When no one answered, I told them all to listen up. "I will never challenge any of you to a fight, but you can bet your ass if you challenge me, it will be in the water. Understand? Sixty marines yelled out, "OORAH, Master Chief."

"Now let's get to work!" I told them.

CHAPTER 16

BACK TO MEXICO

One summer morning while heading to work I could see an Apache helicopter squadron performing exercises off the North Carolina coast. I often marveled at the Apaches because they were lightning fast and packed a big punch with their munitions. The drive into work was a long peaceful one as Camp Lejeune is spread out over 240 square miles. Once on the base, I still had another twenty-five-mile drive to get to work. As I pulled up at the dive locker, I saw my colonel and a few more officers waiting for me.

The first thing out of the commanding officer's mouth was, "Master Diver, we have an Apache down."

Those words are something a master diver never wants to hear, especially when the crash involves a helicopter. Although everyone present was hopeful to find the two pilots alive, I knew better. My time onboard *Salvor* taught me to expect the worse when it comes to aircraft salvage as it is always a sorrow-filled and emotional job. There are two pilots that operate an Apache and normally they are doing at least 180 knots while flying in an aircraft that weighs only 11,000 pounds. I knew right away that two souls would be lost.

I was tasked with my Marines to help in the recovery and salvage of the downed aircraft, which crashed just a few miles offshore. This type of work is not in the job description of a Recon Marine, nor are they trained for it, but I was confident we could get the job done. I grabbed a six-man scuba team and headed down to the marina where a boat was standing by to take us out to the crash site.

The ocean was a bit rough, but nothing for the 30-foot boat we were in. A pilot from the Apache squadron was accompanying us and he had a list of items on his clipboard. At the top of the list, it said: PILOTS. His phone rang and after a very short conversation he crossed out the first line item. I asked him what was up and he said a Navy Explosive Ordnance Team from an offshore aircraft carrier recovered the bodies, but we were tasked with getting all the top-secret equipment off the aircraft and taking photos. I was relieved the pilots were extracted and that we were only tasked to recover equipment.

Once reaching our destination, I noticed the depth of water was no more than fifty feet. I wanted to have an idea of the job site before putting the Marines in, so after anchoring, I slipped into the ocean and there it was right below us. The water was clear enough to see the entire wreckage. The helicopter was barely recognizable, and the blades were stuck in the sand, and extended from the bottom straight up toward the surface. The fuselage was upside down lying on the bottom at an angle, with the tail rotor blades only a couple of feet off the sand. That, and the clear water would make it easy for the Marines to get to the job site once they left the surface.

Back in the boat, I noticed at least one of my Marines getting seasick, and I needed them get moving before all of them fell ill. Seasickness has a habit of being contagious and once one person vomits, others will follow.

My first team had a list of items to salvage, all of which were classified as secret and first and foremost was the pilots' Heads Up Display. I put the first team in the water and told them to follow the rotor blade to the bottom, tapped them on the head and told them to get to work. After twenty minutes, they returned to the surface with all the items on their list.

They were quite proud of themselves, and I have to say so was I. This was their first open ocean dive and they performed like seasoned salvors. Now my seasick corporal was getting worse, but we had two more dives. I asked him if he was sure he was up to being standby diver, and he said he was. The next team was charged with recovering the items on the second half of the list. They were dressed and over the side in a flash. Two taps on their heads and they were gone.

Now the seas were building and we needed to wrap up our recovery efforts, but I still needed to dive and take photos inside the fuselage. The second team of divers were taking their sweet time and finally came up, just short of the maximum time allowed. After getting an okay, I asked them what took so long and they said they found the gear straight away but spent the rest of the time looking at the aircraft. Bone heads!

Now it was my turn. My gear was on and I hopped over the side with the underwater camera in hand. I swam down to the fuselage. but there wasn't enough room to squeeze inside, even though the canopy was gone from the crash. I tried on each side but couldn't squeeze under the wreckage.

Now I was getting frustrated and I tried to lift the fuselage and to my amazement it was as light as a feather. The entire front of the helicopter was carbon fiber composite, and it was nothing to pick it up with one hand. Once inside the cockpit, I started snapping away at all the gauges. Military aircraft have a failsafe system that freezes the gauges, should the aircraft lose power. The photos give the investigators an idea of what happened just prior to the accident. When I was done, I picked the fuselage up, swam out and returned to the surface.

After getting back in the boat I asked the Apache pilot if he was pleased with our work and if there was anything else. To my surprise he said there was something missing. I looked down at his clipboard and written in pen was "wedding bands." I asked what that was about and he exclaimed the pilots were recovered without their watches. He explained that all pilots wore their wedding band on their watch bands so as not to hinder operating the controls.

The rings were lost with the watches during the impact and the squadron wanted to give the families back the rings. I asked him why we didn't do that first, since it was going to take a while to find them. Now with only a single seasick corporal left to dive, I asked him if he was up for the task.

He exclaimed he was feeling really sick but would try. I told him he would be tended with a line. We got him in the water and he vomited straight away and I was about to abort the mission and get back in myself, but he said he wanted to try. I sent him down and told him to give me one pull on the line when he hits the bottom and four pulls when he is ready to come up.

The young corporal was only on the bottom less than a minute and gave us four pulls. I expected he was getting sick on the bottom and needed to abort. As we pulled him up, the first thing we saw was his hand breaking the surface with two rings on his index finger. We all shouted in excitement and pulled him into the boat. I asked him how he found them so quickly.

The corporal said he went down the rotor blade to the sandy bottom and as he looked up, he saw a beam of sunlight glancing off the blade. His eyes followed the light to a small raised sandy patch and both rings were sitting side by side. I rubbed his head and said, "Good job, young man. Let's go home."

Funny how a bit a good luck will make you forget all about being seasick. Everyone was shouting and laughing on the way home, and no one even mentioned it. As soon as the boat pulled into the marina, we were met by the colonel, major, and our first sergeant.

I stepped off the boat with the pilot and the colonel asked us how it went. I replied, "Job complete," and the pilot confirmed that we did a great job. The colonel looked surprised and I laughed at him and I asked, "What did you expect?"

He said it was just that Marines had never done a job like that and I replied, "Now they've done it."

The first sergeant then reminded everyone that the following day I was going on leave. In fact, I would be traveling to Cabo San Lucas, Mexico. Then all eyes shifted to the squadron pilot, as if he would be the deciding factor on my annual pilgrimage to Mexico. He said that all recovery efforts were one hundred percent complete, and that mobile diving salvage Unit 2 from Norfolk would recover the aircraft. He looked at me and said, "Have a nice vacation."

I had a very satisfying smile on my face the whole day while flying down to Mexico. It had been four years since the tiger shark incident, but since then I'd learned a lot about blue water spearfishing and was comfortable again. After my first year, the owners of the boat, Capt. Mike and Miss Sherry, offered me my own trip each year and from that point on I had my own crew and we visited them annually. Capt. Mike liked to have me onboard because I was a US Coast Guard licensed captain and to visit the islands there was a Mexican regulation that two captains were required to be onboard.

Our routine each year was the same. We would all arrive from different parts of the world, stow our gear on the boat, and take Capt. Mike and Miss Sherry out for dinner. At dinner we would all catch up and most importantly Capt. Mike would give us the fish reports and our game plan for the ten-day trip.

He explained to us that on the last trip, which ended just the previous week, they found most of the quality yellowfin tuna up on the northern end of San Benedicto Island. My first question was: "Wow, how were the sharks up there, Captain?"

"Well, I'm not going to lie to you, there are a bunch. But that's also where the tuna are, so we are heading there first."

After a day at sea, we woke up to a beautiful sunrise and in front of us the volcanic island of San Benedicto. The captain decided to circumnavigate the island and look for fish using his side scan sonar and, just as he had explained the day before, the north end of the island was alive with fish. Side scan showed baitfish stacked up and large tuna below them. In the blue sky, thousands of birds showed us the way. The captain had been here many times in the past and his anchorage spot was marked on the GPS chart plotter, so it didn't take long to anchor and shut down the main engines.

All of us were on the back deck of the boat getting ready and the moment the engines were shut down the sharks arrived behind the swim platform and under the boat. There were numerous seven to ten-foot whalers cruising on the surface right behind the boat and two very large dusky sharks that looked about twelve feet long. My dive partner that morning would be my great friend Brandi, who was absolutely fearless around sharks, and the horde lurking behind the boat did nothing to deter her in the least. I hopped into the clear blue water first and before the bubbles could even clear, I saw a large tiger shark swimming directly toward me. This time I was prepared and swam directly at her and she swam away.

Large predators are used to being aggressive, but don't like being on the defensive. It makes them uncomfortable. As I was waiting for Brandi to get in the water, one of the other divers asked me how it was. I told him a sane person wouldn't get in. In fact, all the others chose to stay in the boat that morning. Once Brandi joined me, we swam together toward the point. I noticed the further we got away from the boat, the fewer sharks we saw.

By now the Mexican deckhands had the panga (small boat) in the water and were following us at a safe distance. The water was just magical, baitfish everywhere, and birds were diving into the water around us trying to grab an easy meal. As I looked below, I saw a shelf at about sixty feet and then another down around ninety feet before it dropped away into the abyss. Then I saw a school of ten to fifteen large yellowfin tunas, all over two hundred pounds, swim up on the first shelf then up to the second shelf before chasing an eight-foot whaler. They were nipping on the shark's tailfins aggravating it. As soon as the shark would turn to go after the tunas, they would turn and swim back down into the depths.

Brandi and I watched this interaction repeatedly and finally I told her that the next time I see them coming up the shelf I'm going to be waiting on the second shelf for them. As if on cue, the big tunas once again swam up the shelf and I dove as fast as I could to get to the sixty-foot shelf before they did. I landed on a large rock on the bottom and watched them below me. For some reason, they now decided to take their time. Finally, they must have thought the coast was clear and swam directly toward me.

Blending into the bottom, I laid there motionless with my gun stretched out in front of me. It's not hard to shoot a two-hundred-pound fish, but the larger ones are always in the rear. My lungs were exploding and I wouldn't be able to hold my breath much longer when the biggest tuna in the group decided to come closer for a look. My massive tuna gun exploded and the shaft hit the tuna in one gill plate and out the other.

As I swam back up toward Brandi, I could see the onslaught of sharks racing toward my prize. Usually, sharks were wary about attacking a big fish because they know even a tuna has enough power to cripple a shark. They will wait until they know the fish is in trouble before trying to take a bite. The tuna was doing a good job staying clear of the horde of sharks that were coming in, right up to the point where a tiger shark showed up and bit the tuna in half. The sound it made as its teeth went through flesh and bone was incredibly eerie. It swallowed the tuna's head portion first, while spitting out my shaft. Before any smaller sharks could race in for leftovers, the tiger ate the rear section too, swallowing it like a sardine.

When a 240-pound tuna gets bit in half, it creates a huge blood ball and now at least thirty sharks were looking for the host. The last place you want to be is in the water above a massive blood ball with sharks trying to find something to sink their teeth into. Both Brandi and I shouted for the panga and before it arrived, at least ten sharks were all around us. But we held our ground and pushed them away as a team. After we jumped into the panga, we both laid in the bottom of the boat for a moment, looking up into the sky and just laughed at one another before giving each other a big hug.

After returning to the main boat and telling our story, we decided to eat lunch. Brandi was a professional photographer, so she moved around the boat taking photos of everyone and everything. The captain decided to move the boat around to the back side of the island to see if there were fewer sharks. It was the same spot where four years earlier, I almost became dinner for a sixteen-foot tiger shark.

I noticed one shark on my morning dive with Brandi which had a heavy red monofilament line attached to a hook in a whaler's mouth. The line was as long as the whaler and I could see that the hook was rusting in the corner of the shark's mouth. I felt a little bad for the poor thing swimming around the ocean dragging a leash. When Brandi and I slipped into the water in the bay the first thing I saw was that very same shark. I tried several times to grab the monofilament, but each time I got close the shark swam away. The bay didn't seem to have as many sharks as the northern end, so Brandi and I swam away from the boat. The bay was glass calm and I could see a nice fat wahoo swimming toward Brandi on the surface.

I picked my head up and the panga was close by but I motioned for them to get closer. Although sharks are not likely to attack a two-hundred-pound tuna, they will jump on a wahoo in a fraction of a second. Brandi lined the wahoo up and squeezed the trigger and the shaft impacted right behind its head and it raced off. I saw a few whalers now passing us to get to Brandi's fish, but she was not giving up and pulled as hard as she could to muscle the fish closer. Two whalers were closing in on her wahoo, so I dove down to escort her wahoo to the surface. Sharks are very opportunistic, but the moment it looks like they might have to battle for their meal they usually think twice.

We returned to the mother boat and took some photos of Brandi's fish and decided to have a beer. As the other divers came back to the boat, they expressed their concerns about the numbers of whalers and whether any fish could be landed. Capt. Mike stepped out on the back deck and said he'd heard enough and after dark he would be moving the boat over to Socorro Island some twenty-six miles away. Surely, he said there will be fewer sharks there. After a great dinner, a few beers, and a beautiful sunset, the engines roared to life and we were underway for Socorro Island.

The Captain would cruise slowly throughout the night so we would arrive first thing in the morning and that way would not waste any time. We all awoke to the sound of the diesel engines slowing down and I grabbed a cup of coffee and went for a look outside. In front of the boat was the famous Cabo Pierce of Socorro Island. Cabo Pierce is a finger that points out into the ocean with three hundred-foot cliffs bordering water that dropped to a depth of three hundred feet. It is a magnet for large tuna to come in and feed on baitfish. From the birds flying overhead we knew they would be here. We all scrambled to get into the water after Capt. Mike anchored. As I slipped into the beautiful clear warm water, to my amazement I saw that same shark with the red monofilament line hanging out of his mouth. It had followed us, along with many of its mates, twenty-six miles during the night.

Today I would be paired with another diver and we swam away from the boat toward the sea to get away from the sharks. The Cabo Pierce finger extends out into the ocean at least a half mile and we stayed near the surface mingling with millions of blue fusilier's fishes. It's not as boring when you are in the midst of so many baitfish and besides, it was the tuna's number one source of food. I saw the fusiliers bolt for cover, then turned to see a massive school of tuna coming our way, hundreds upon hundreds of tunas.

The ones in the front were 100-150 pounds and there was no end in sight of the school it was so immense. My dive partner was down about thirty feet from the surface and the tuna parted around him on both sides. But as they were going around him the school continued to get closer and closer to him. He could no longer wait for the end of the school and made an easy shot on a 150-pound fish, and in a flash the school of tuna and my dive partner were gone. I picked my head up to see the panga was dispatched to get my partner and the closest thing to me was the mother boat about three hundred yards away.

Great, I thought to myself, *I have been in this position before. I better start swimming with a purpose.* I could barely see the bottom below, but the fusiliers were returning. Then the first two sharks arrived and one of them was the damn thing I felt sorry for with the red line. Two sharks turned into four, then four turned into eight, and before I knew it, there were more than I could count.

Two divers can fend off many sharks working as a team, but a single diver cannot. I was pushing them off with the tip of my gun and yelling for the rescue boat to get me out of the water. Then I started to panic as the sharks started ramming me from the back and now the sides and front.

Shark's ram and bump you because their taste buds are in their nose and they are trying to decipher if you are food. Then I went from panic to rage and decided if I was going to die, I was going to hurt as many of them as I could. They were all over me smashing me from all angles, some with their tails flipping out of the water.

I hit a few so hard they backed away immediately and then

a few more got smashed in the face from my speargun. Just then when I thought the end would be close, the panga pulled up and I was yanked out of the water. Everyone in the boat saw me in the center of the shark frenzy and thought for sure I was bitten during the mayhem.

Moral of the story is: never quit, never ever quit!

CHAPTER 17

COMPROMISE IT IF YOU CAN

I was anxious to get back to Camp Lejeune and catch up with my Marines. My first day back at work started with a yellow sticky note on my desk that said, "Welcome Home, Master Diver. Please come see me, Colonel."

I walked through a grove of trees toward the headquarters building, and as I was crossing the parking lot, a car shot past me going way too fast. The driver then slammed on his brakes. The car door swung open, and an overweight major stepped out screaming at me, something about me not saluting his car.

I said I'm not required to salute a car unless it has a flag with a star present. Then the major demanded to know who I worked for. I calmly said I was heading there now and politely told him to follow me. The colonel's office was just inside the main door on the left. I walked in with the major hot on my heels and said, "Good morning, colonel. This major would like to speak to you, in regard to me not saluting his car while he was speeding through our parking lot."

The colonel's face went from happy go lucky, to utter disgust, in a fraction of a second. I don't think the major had a chance to say one word, before he was thrown out, and told never to cut through our parking lot again. With that, the colonel sat down, offered me a cup of coffee, and asked how my leave was. I smiled and told him, "Well, I almost became shark food."

He laughed and said, "I'm glad you didn't. The general wants to see us. He has a mission for you."

Later that morning, we were sitting in front of our general, and I was very curious about what sort of mission he had in mind. He asked if I had been watching the news, then explained to us that Turkey and Syria were on the verge of war. The conflict between the two countries had escalated, and they were shooting missiles and munitions back and forth across the border. Our government had decided to attempt to cool down the conflict, by staging a major training mission on the coast, between the two countries.

Therefore, they would not be able to shoot at one another without shooting over the top of us, and of course that would be forbidden. "How can I help?" I asked.

"Do you know what 'pre-position ships' are?"

I said they are military transports, camouflaged as commercial freighters. They are approximately a thousand feet long, and filled with enough weapons to start a war, and they normally travel in sets of three.

He said that was right, then he asked if force recon could provide underwater security for those vessels, by sweeping them for explosives on a daily basis. He went on to say that two ships would be at anchor, one ship would be at the pier, and they would rotate. He passed photos across his desk and showed me the pier.

I told him the hardest vessel to sweep would always be the one that is pier-side. The general then showed me photos of the surrounding area, and I noticed a concrete pillbox sitting atop a hill, overlooking the ocean and pier. I asked the general if we could use it, or a portion of it, since we would have to bring a transportable recompression chamber with us. He said we could, then told me my command wouldn't be going on the mission, just me and my recon Marines, and we would work directly for him.

We landed at Incirlik, Turkey Air Force Base with all our gear onboard a massive C-5 Galaxy Aircraft. After loading our gear on a tractor trailer, the recon team climbed into three Humvees, and we followed the trailer down to the port about an hour away. We pulled up to our new home, the concrete pillbox, and started to off-load, when that very same fat major from the parking lot incident ran out, demanding my men stop.

I walked up behind him and asked if I could help, and when he turned and saw me, his face turned red with anger. He announced himself as the supply officer and said that the pillbox was already taken to store our meals and supplies, and we would not be staying there.

I politely told the major to hold that thought, that I would be right back. I walked to the nearby Humvee, found my backpack, and pulled out the cell phone the general had given me, with his number pre-programed in it. The general picked up on the first ring, and asked what was wrong, and I explained the situation.

"Let me speak to the major," he replied.

I happily walked back to him and handed him the phone. "I think this is for you, major."

It was a very short conversation. After hanging up the major asked me how much room we needed and said he would be happy to share the pillbox. But as the major walked away, he mumbled, "Who the hell does he think he is?"

I replied loudly, "Excuse me, major. I am a master chief/ master diver, and the only one in the U.S. Marine Corps. My chain of command is the fine general you just spoke to, then the commandant himself. Maybe you would like to speak to him next."

"That won't be necessary," he grudgingly replied and moved on.

There seems to be a lot of jealousy and animosity in the military toward any special teams, regardless of which service they represent. Some such observers see divers or recon as teams that spend their time working out or walking around in shorts and swimming every day in the beautiful ocean. The reality was that we had a far more grueling schedule than any of these critics within the military.

I had twenty-four chips with numbers on them 1-24, each representing an hour of the day. Each day I would reach in a bag and grab three chips. If the chips were 4, 16 and 22, we would dive at 0400 am 1600 pm and 2200 pm.

This way if anyone was watching us and wanted to do harm to one of the ships, we didn't have a routine that they could exploit. No one, not even me, knew what time we would be diving the following day. It didn't take long for the other Marines to figure out how hard we were working, because we were diving seven days a week and twenty-four hours a day.

Some days we had to sleep all day to operate at night. One day we were sleeping after being up all night, and a few Marines from the supply department thought it would be funny to blast their stereo inside the pillbox. I got up and walked to the opposite side of the pillbox and asked them politely to turn it down. No sooner had I returned to my cot when they turned it back up.

They might have been playing some game, but we were not. This time I walked back over with two of my staff sergeants. We were all issued automatic knives, mine was opened the moment we returned to the stereo, and I cut the power cord. The owner of the stereo said he could fix that by putting another plug on. Then my staff sergeant picked up the stereo and smashed it into a thousand pieces on the concrete floor, then said: "Let me see you fix that."

If that wasn't enough to deter people from messing with us, every now and then, the general would stop by in the evening and ask us how we were all holding up. He would even grab a "meal ready to eat" and sit down with us. Of course, if he were there, a half dozen senior officers accompanied him. But the general recognized we were busting our asses, and what we were doing had a significant impact. Without us the mission would be a bust.

The mission was to stop the fighting between Syria and Turkey, and the presence of the three ships was a deterrent, because the two countries couldn't shoot over the ships without facing repercussions from the US military. However, without the protection of the ships by the Marine Recon divers, who worked around the clock, the ships would have had to stay out at sea.

The waters off the coast of Turkey were crystal clear. It made our job of sweeping an anchored 1000-foot vessel an easy task. But the vessel tied up pier-side would take us twice as long, since the visibility in the harbor was much worse.

One day I pulled two chips for the ships at anchorage: 1200 and 1600. Plan was to dive on the first ship, then wait offshore and dive on the second, before returning to shore. On this particular day, the sun was shining and the ocean was calm. We had about an hour to relax before the next dive, so we let the boat drift and my Marines wanted to have a free- diving contest. We lowered a weight down fifty feet and I said, "Let's see who can get there." To my surprise all of them made it.

"Okay, let's lower it down to 75 feet," I said.

Everyone in special teams is highly competitive, alpha males from birth. All of them tried their hardest, but only one was able to make it to the bottom of the line, staff sergeant (Scott). When Scott returned to the surface all the marines were screaming at me to top that. I made my dive and sat on the weighted line at seventy-five feet and concentrated for over a minute, and then had a good "poo". After returning to the surface, we all were laughing hysterically. The moment we all jumped back into the boat, I saw the telltale sign of a submarine going by, just below the surface. I pointed it out to my Marines. "You see those four semi-circle wakes? That's a submarine going by."

I jumped behind the controls of the boat, started it up, and we leapt ahead of the submarine. I stopped and told them to have a look over the side. We all put our masks on and dunked our heads in the water, to watch the submarine glide by. I had a lot of experience working on our submarines. I knew it wasn't one of ours. As it went by, I heard its sonar pinging. Submarine sonar can cause serious hearing damage for any divers in the area. For U.S. military divers to be in the water with an operating submarine nearby, the sonar must be no more than ten percent power.

Every evening that we weren't diving at 1900, I was expected to attend a meeting with all the senior people on our base. Normally at the end of the meeting the tactical officer in command, a colonel, would ask if anyone had anything to add. On this night, I raised my hand. "Please tell whichever Navy is operating the submarine, not to use more than 10 percent power on their active sonar. It could hurt us."

The tent turned quiet for a few moments, then the colonel

said there was no submarines operating in this area. "That is incorrect, sir," I responded. "We saw it, and it's not a U.S. asset."

As the meeting broke up, I was pulled aside by the colonel and several other senior officers. They asked me not to call it a submarine, that I should refer to it as an underwater anomaly. "You can call it what you like, but it's a non-U.S. submarine. I saw it."

The colonel then tasked me to dive at the same location where we supposedly saw the submarine, to insure it was not an underwater mountain range or some other anomaly.

"You must be a genius, sir. You think there's an underwater mountain in the center of an anchorage."

He didn't like my response, and I didn't like his order. But a direct order is just that, and I stormed out of the tent. The next day I grabbed a six-man scuba team, and we went to that very same spot. We put a weighted line down and found the bottom at 145 feet. I told my divers to stop when they saw the bottom, and not to go any deeper than 130 feet. The dive only took fifteen minutes. The divers reported they saw nothing.

On the way back, while I was driving the boat, everyone was carrying on as they usually did, laughing and joking with each other. But then I noticed one of the sergeants who was diving, was starting to slump over to one side. I stopped the boat to ask if he was okay, and immediately saw it in his eyes, and he said he could not move from the neck down.

I told my dive medic to grab him, then I pinned the throttles down as far as they would go. We had a few miles to go so, I radioed in and told the base we had a medical emergency, and to stand by. As we pulled in, a Humvee was waiting to get the sergeant to the recompression chamber. It took less than two minutes to get him to the chamber, and we slid him in with a back board, and pressed him down to 165 feet.

The sergeant responded almost immediately, so we moved him up to sixty feet and put him on oxygen. About that time, the general walked in. He asked what had happened. I told him one of the Marines suffered an arterial gas embolism, but he would be okay. The general asked how this could happen, and I explained we saw a foreign submarine, but the colonel wanted me to confirm it was not an underwater anomaly.

"Did you tell him that was fucking stupid?" he asked.

"Yes, sir, I did."

He asked me to describe the submarine, and I told him it wasn't one of ours, because the planes were forward of the conning tower, and ours are built into the conning tower. Planes are like wings that protrude from the sides of submarines, and control the angle of the dive, and other maneuvers. Before walking out he looked at me and said, "Master Chief, if you get the opportunity to compromise it, then do so."

"Roger that, sir."

I checked on my sergeant several times throughout the night, and he seemed to be fine, but he would be disqualified from diving for the next thirty days because of the accident. We had a Navy Scorpion unit helping protect the pre-positioned ships, and with them was an anti-submarine warfare team. The following day in a meeting, the team asked if we could deploy sonobuoys for them. A sonobuoy is a passive ping system which can locate, and then transmit, a submarine's position to an overhead satellite. They had twelve sonobuoys they wanted us to deploy at different locations around the anchorage, and several miles beyond it.

I told them I needed to speak to my general, and when I did so, he asked me what my plan B was?

"Plan B, sir?"

"What happens if you get caught? You could be killed or you could be captured. We have no jurisdiction in Turkish waters."

I asked the general if we had Navy assets offshore and he said there was an entire battle group. "Sir, Plan B, if we are caught, we will travel west toward the battle group, and scuttle the boat prior to getting apprehended, then go on our Drager rebreathers. We can then stay underwater for four hours while continuing to swim west. We will then surface and radio our location on the secure network for a pickup.

He smiled and said, "You should've been a Marine."

My Marines were well trained for a task like the one we were about to undertake, but nothing in my job description or training, prepared me for this type of operation that could involve combat at sea. We were to deploy at time 00:00 and as we were getting ready and checking our weapons, my phone rang. It was my colonel back in North Carolina, and he asked, "Master Chief, what are you thinking?"

"Just a little boat ride, sir."

The colonel said that the general had informed him about the operation, and he just wanted to wish me luck and Godspeed. Then he asked to speak to my staff sergeant. I handed the phone to Scott, and the conversation was very short. I only heard Scott say, "Oorah, sir," and hang up. He went back to checking his rifle, and I asked what the colonel wanted.

"He said, if anything happens to you, for me not to come back."

Scott knew I had never done anything like this, and just said, "We got you, Master Chief. You drive the boat, and we'll take care of the rest."

We loaded the boat just before midnight with me, four Force Recon Marines, five Dragers, and enough weapons to start a war. The Marine Corps did not skimp on our Rigid Inflatable Boat. It was a very capable twenty-six-foot boat, with twin engines that were both agile and fast. If we were to get caught, it would have to be by something very special indeed. We left the safety of our camp and started out. The boat was totally blacked out, and even our navigation systems had subdued lighting. There was also no moon or stars out, just total blackness. It would be hard to see us.

The boat quickly came up on a plane, and we were heading for our first sonobuoy drop site, which was the furthest one offshore. We had a string of sonobuoys to deploy on the edge of the continental shelf. Once they were in place, we would move inshore to deploy the remaining four. As we placed the eighth buoy, I noticed white water coming directly for us, about three hundred yards away. The wake was being created by a coastal patrol craft that was about one hundred feet long.

I yelled out for the guys to get down and pinned the throttles as fast as the boat could go. But the patrol craft had momentum and was quickly closing in on us. It slowed momentarily and two smaller boats pulled out from behind it. We now had three craft pursuing us. Although we were faster, it would be difficult to outrun three boats. An amplified voice ordered us to stop.

I kept going, zig zagging, and as the boats got closer and closer, I prayed no one would start shooting. I knew at the first shot, whether it was a warning shot, or one aimed toward us, that my Marines would let loose with a barrage of fire power. All of their weapons were loaded with 40mm grenade launchers, which would destroy the small foreign boats and kill them all. U.S. doctrine for small teams being assaulted is "overwhelming fire power for a short duration."

The boats were moving in on either side. They were intent on ramming us. As we leapt out in front of the other boats, one split to the left and the other to the right, with the patrol boat behind us. Each one had three armed soldiers aboard, pointing their weapons at us. I realized they were going to try to ram us simultaneously from either side. I needed to do something quickly.

I noticed the patrol boat was falling back, and that gave me an idea. I told my guys to hold on and get down. I pulled the throttles back to stop our boat, as if there was a mechanical problem. The other boats were bearing down at us, moving at thirty knots. Two seconds before impact, I slammed our boat into reverse. The two foreign boats narrowly missed our bow, and collided head on with one another. Bodies seemed to be flying in all directions from the collision. We didn't hang around to see if anyone was hurt. Instead, we fled the scene at over forty knots.

The other four sonobuoy drop sites were on a direct line back to the coast, and I told the Marines to get ready to drop them, but we would not be slowing down. All of them were deployed in their intended location, Now with all of them marked on the navigational chart plotter, I could see a pattern that resembled a funnel. The Navy guys had us deploy the sonobuoys in a manner that would squeeze the submarine to a confined lane over the shallowest part of the anchorage, with only one way in, and only one way out.

The following day we were getting ready to dive on our ships when the Navy team showed up at our boat. I invited them to step aboard, and then I showed them the twelve marks on the navigation plotter, where we deployed the sonobuoys. When I asked them about the pattern and the narrow lane, they smiled. I told them when they get an active contact, to call me on the radio. They acknowledged by saying my four favorite words, "Roger that, Master Chief."

As we pulled away from the pier, I saw a Humvee racing toward us. It was the colonel, and a few of the officers on his staff. I guessed that neither the general nor the Navy Scorpion team, had felt the need to brief him on our midnight excursion. He was quite upset that he wasn't informed about it, until the Turkish Navy caught him by surprise and accused him of espionage.

He also said that several Turkish soldiers were hurt in the incident. He asked me how in the world was he ever going to answer them, and I replied, "Deny, deny, deny."

"That is not going to be good enough, Master Chief. I want to know who authorized you to do the mission."

I laughed and said, "I never said we did it, but if we did, the answer to your question is above your pay grade."

Later that same day, I got a call on the radio from the Navy team. "Contact coming in now." We were just finishing off a dive on one of the ships at anchor, when I turned the boat and headed for the shallow pinch point. I shut the engines down so the submarine couldn't hear us. The water depth was only 110 feet, which is very shallow for a submarine. I knew the crew of the submarine would be nervous operating at that depth, and hopefully they would raise her periscope.

The Scorpion team had very good real-time satellite coverage of the anchorage area. We could see the telltale semi-circle wakes coming from a half mile away, and I was sure the satellites were now focusing in on the submarine. We were sitting quietly, and when she was only a boat length away, she raised her periscope. I started the engines and kept up with the sub. When the scope panned toward us, we all flipped the submarine the bird. Then it disappeared below the surface. We stayed over the top of the submarine for several miles while they tried to exit to deep water. The whole time our command post was watching via satellite.

Getting compromised is every submariner's worst nightmare, also their most shameful moment. But for us, we were proud to prove that yes, there was a foreign submarine prowling inside our operational area.

CHAPTER 18

SAVE A LIFE

The day after we chased the submarine out of the harbor, I woke to the sound of voices. I knew it wasn't my men because we didn't get back from diving until 0300. The smell of fresh coffee filled the air as well. That was something new. Since being in Turkey, we'd only had instant coffee. The smell of brewed coffee was enough to get me up.

I walked outside to see the general sitting and talking to a few officers on his staff. He had a big thermos and a couple of coffee cups. The general invited me for a sit and poured me a cup. It was like heaven.

"This is real coffee, General."

He smiled and said, "Yes, one of the perks of being in charge."

"Must be nice," I responded.

He smiled. "You know what is nice, Master Chief? Having you and your Marines here. You guys did a great job with that submarine, and I want you to know I appreciate it. Take your team up to Incirlik Air Force Base for the next 24 hours and enjoy yourself. Come see me when you get back. I need a favor."

I walked back into the pillbox and shouted for everyone to get up. Before anyone could complain, I said: "We got the day off. Get dressed, we're going to Incirlik."

Only a solder or sailor can truly appreciate the gesture the general bestowed upon us. None of us had so much as a good hot shower, haircut, or even a clean uniform after stepping into Turkey, much less a beer.

Typically, when you go on a deployment like this, you only have two uniforms. The one you arrive in and the one you go home in. We converged onto the Air Force Base looking like a bunch of cavemen. You could see the disgust in the faces of the Air Force service members when we walked in, and we took over the gym to get cleaned up.

All of us had our going home uniform with us, and we bagged the ones we were wearing, after getting cleaned up. We dropped the dirty uniforms off to get cleaned, got haircuts, then everyone split up, with the agreement to meet at the base club by 2100. It was nice to feel like a regular person again, even if it was for just one day. By midnight, we all returned to the safe confines of our concrete box and had our first great night's sleep since arriving in Turkey.

I woke up the next morning feeling like a different person, a clean one with a fresh haircut and shave. I walked over to see the general, bringing staff sergeant Scott along. The general liked me and my men, and he would joke around with us like one of the boys. But it was clear he was a general.

He said, "Master Chief, being as you like playing soldier boy so much, I wonder if you and your Marines would do me a favor? We have Marine Corps Fast Company teams stationed onboard each pre-position ship, to provide security. Each team has approximately fifteen Marines. Can you test their skillsets?"

I looked at my staff sergeant and he gave me a slight nod, then I asked the general about the rules of engagement. "You test whichever ship you like between the hours of 2200-0000."

"That hardly seems fair, General, the Fast Marines only have to pay attention for 120 minutes," I responded.

"Well, we want to make it challenging for you as well."

Staff Sergeant Scott looked at me and just nodded, but I could see wheels turning behind his eyes. We went back to our pillbox and called the men together. The consensus was, they wanted to make a statement on the very first night.

We planned to hit an offshore ship at anchor, and we would do it by diving Drager from 500 yards away. Then we would board the ship by walking up the massive anchor chain, and through the ships huge chain pipe. I added one more caveat. "We'll board that ship at 2200. So, we will splash at 2100 and stage our gear on the anchor chain and wait for the assault."

Eight of us entered the water at 2100 and I navigated the team to the ship. We had ample time to remove our Dragers and tie them to the anchor chain. At 2200:00, we went up the chain. To our surprise, we found two Fast Company Marines eating peanut butter and crackers. Not only that, but their weapons were at least twenty feet away.

After we tie-wrapped them, four of us sprinted to the bridge, and the other four sprinted for the engine room. In short measure we took over the ship. All fifteen Marines were tie-wrapped. I called into Command Control, and announced:

"Raider 1 has control of Williams at 2204."

During the briefing on the exercise the next day, the commander of the Fast Company Marines was outraged. He threw his helmet and acted like a little kid, exclaiming that we cheated. I asked how do you suppose we cheated, sir? He said coming up the anchor chain was dangerous and we should have known that it was off-limits. Then the general piped in and told the commander to stop his whining. Recon won fair and square and with a much smaller force.

The commander, however, wasn't done and challenged us again, stating we would never be able to duplicate our efforts from the previous night. The general gave me a look and then asked, "Master Chief?"

"Sure thing. Tomorrow night, same rules of engagement."

Everyone agreed that this time we needed to come up with something original. There were only two ways to board the two ships at sea: the anchor chain, and up the gangway. We knew they would be heavily guarded, so we focused on the pier-side asset. The head of the pier was guarded by fifteen Fast Company Marines, and there was another team of fifteen onboard the ship. We suspected the Fast Company commander would focus his efforts on the ships at anchor, since the ship at pier side had twice as many Marines guarding it.

But that's the ship we decided to assault. We would take on both teams of fifteen with our eight-man recon team. The plan was going to be twofold: first, we would create a diversion at the head of the pier, large enough that the Marines on the ship would have to assist. Then we would overpower the remaining Marines on the ship.

For the diversion, we would use two of our Marines swimming in Drager to the head of the pier, then exiting the water, and climbing onto the pier. They would not be carrying any weapons, but each would have well-hidden flash bangs. Their job was to take out all fifteen Marines, and themselves with the flash bangs. My two Marines would be sacrificial pawns for the other six of us to get close enough to the ship, and assault it.

Every day the base quartermasters moved containers from the supply depot, down to the pier, twenty-four hours a day. They used huge tractors to transport the containers. We approached the quartermasters and asked them if they would like to play a role in our security exercise, and they jumped at the chance.

We had a twenty-foot container that we would use as a Trojan horse. Six of us would be inside it. The tractor would pick us up at 2130, transport us down the pier, and place us in front of the ship's gangway. We would all be wearing coveralls over our uniforms and hardhats as a disguise. That would allow us to get up the gangway without a fight. We also drilled a few holes in our container, to keep an eye on things once we were on the pier.

We launched our two Recon Marines on Drager. They were to swim 500 yards underwater then stage underneath the pier, but not climb up onto the pier until 2200:00. The quartermaster tractor operator came over, picked us up, and got us through the Fast Company's security checkpoint on the pier. He then set us down in front of the ship's gang way at time 2155.

Five minutes later, right on cue, we heard shouts down the pier, ordering my Marines to get down on the ground. All fifteen Marines had them surrounded, and as inexperienced soldiers often do, they all got too close. When both Flash Bangs went off, the Command Control Referee called all fifteen fast Company Marines dead, plus my two Recon Marines. The Commander of the Marine Fast Company was on the ship and sent five Marines to lend a hand on the pier. We saw them run down the gangway as we peered through the holes in the container.

We opened the container, and I sent two of my disguised Marines up the gang way, and one was holding a third flashbang behind his back. The Marines on the ship were all trying to see what was happening on the pier and were not paying attention to the threat in coveralls walking up the gangway.

The third flashbang went off at the feet of the commander and his men, and the remaining four of us raced up the gangway. The Command Control referee called the ten Fast Company Marines on the ship, plus my two Recon Marines "dead". Now there was no protection on the ship. Two of my Marines went to engineering, while Staff Sergeant Scott and myself raced toward the ship's bridge. Once on the bridge, I let Scott call it in: "Command Control, this is Raider 1, we have control of Bobo, time 2205."

The commander of the Fast Company, who was actually a Lt. Colonel by rank, was now on the pier arguing with the Command Control referees. His argument was that we acted like terrorist, instead of marines, and used suicide bombers to dispatch his men. My reply was, "we were never asked not to act like terrorists," as I walked away to join my men. We were removing our borrowed coveralls on the pier by our container when I heard the Lt. Colonel call out: "Piece of shit, sailor."

I walked up to him with Scott on my heels and said, "What I am is a master chief/master diver, the only one in the U.S. Marine Corps. You, lieutenant colonel, are a dime a dozen and a poor leader."

Before he could come back with a reply, the general walked up and said, "He's correct, now stand down." The general asked the senior referee if it was fair, and how did seven Recon Marines and one master chief take a ship so quickly, with thirty Fast Company Marines guarding it.

The referee answered, "Deception, speed, and timing. It was a great plan, and an even better execution."

The commander admitted that he couldn't have done anything better, and then the general asked, "Master Chief?"

I called Staff Sergeant Scott over, as he was the true expert, and asked him to work with the Fast Company teams in the days ahead, to get them up to speed. The general just smiled at me and said, "You should have been a Marine."

The next day during our nightly meeting, the Fast Company commander apologized to me, and then thanked me. But I overheard the Navy Scorpion commander say we could never do that to his unit. The Scorpion Unit operated a satellite security system that provided oversight and protection for the pre-position ships in port. It had a command control trailer, four twenty-six-foot fast boats, and several automated weapon systems that were all uplinked to dedicated satellites. It was quite a high-tech operation, but I was certain that it was as vulnerable as the ships with their Marine Fast Company teams.

After the meeting, the general called me aside and asked for a favor. "Master Chief, can you and your men lose one? The Fast Company teams took a massive blow to their ego, and they really need to win one."

"General my guys are in the business of not losing." Then I agreed that it was fine, as long as he allowed me to take out the Scorpion team. He asked me why, and I told him I overhead the Scorpion commander say we could never overcome their security.

The general nodded and shook my hand. "I'd like to see that."

People have a tendency to become complacent, and believe they are untouchable. For our demonstration, we were going to teach the Navy Scorpion team a little humility. A few days later, seven of us went on Drager from more than five hundred yards away at time 2100, to assault the Bobo on the pier again.

We had two very special missions. The first was for five Recon Marines to assault the Bobo on the pier and die in a very dramatic death at the hands of the two Fast Companies. Staff Sergeant Scott and I would swim under the pier, and to the outboard side of the Bobo, and hide out and wait. The last recon diver, Brownee, who was a sergeant, was to drive a blacked out fourteen-foot rubber boat, with a twenty-five-horsepower motor, as fast as possible to the rear of the Bobo. He would be ranting and raving that he was going to blow up the ship while doing tight circles with the boat.

Everything began as planned at 2200:00, and because a boat was threatening the security of the ship, I knew a Scorpion boat would respond. I heard yelling and screaming on the pier, as five of my Marines were confronted. Then Brownee's rubber boat showed up. I couldn't have picked a better Marine for this job. Brownee was a natural born wise ass, and was screaming at the top of his lungs, that he was going to blow up the ship.

A Scorpion boat with a driver and two security guards, with weapons drawn responded within minutes. They were bellowing for my Marine to shut his boat down, but Brownee drew them in closer and closer to us. Finally, he stopped the boat and both guards were on the starboard side, pointing their rifles at him. He was howling like a mad man, and the three of them didn't hear Scott and I coming over the port side. We held our knives up to their throats and disarmed them and tie-wrapped them both before the driver of the boat even knew what was going on. The Navy Scorpion team wasn't expecting a security drill, and so the weapons onboard were locked and loaded.

We put the two security guards down below, taped their mouths shut, and tie-wrapped the boat driver. Brownee put our Dragers into the rubber boat, and released it, as he joined us on Scorpion 1. Scott could be quite menacing when he wanted to be, and the boat driver quickly gave us the location of the command trailer, which was code named "Crafty Cheese."

We pulled up to the hidden Scorpion dock, which had four Navy security personnel guarding the pier and trailer. We disarmed and tie-wrapped them all, and slid an empty satchel, representing an explosive, under the trailer door. We then returned to Scorpion 1. The Navy Scorpion team and our Command Control Center shared the same radio net, and I placed this call: "Crafty Cheese, Scorpion One."

"Go ahead, Scorpion One."

"Scorpion One is now Raider One. You have a bomb under your trailer. Have a nice evening."

Crafty Cheese had no idea if the threat was real or not, and as we were pulling away from the dock, sailors were scattering out of the trailer like cockroaches. We pulled back into our boat's normal berth and released the sailors onboard Scorpion One. We said no hard feelings, but they were pissed. I figured there would be some flack the next day, but I barely got out of the shower when one of my Marines said my presence was requested at the Command Center now.

I heard a clamor of shouts before I even entered the tent. Apparently, the Navy commander had no prior knowledge that their own security was being tested and was quite upset. Then there was the issue of us disarming the sailors, who had loaded weapons, and scaring the shit out of the technicians in the trailer. The general let everyone vent and took it all in, before finally saying, "Did everyone learn something tonight? Good, now let's go to bed."

Walking out of the tent, he put his hand on my shoulder and squeezed, which I took to mean, good job!

Our time in Turkey was coming to an end, and we spent the entire day loading up the recompression chamber and all our gear onto a tractor trailer. Now with the job done, we were all enjoying our last dinner in Turkey, when the phone in my pocket rang.

I saw it was a Turkish number.

I answered, and on the other end was an Air Force physician from Incirlik, he asked if we had a recompression chamber. He said he had a young female lieutenant who may have decompression sickness from a recreational dive. She was in a very bad way, and he doubted she would make it. I told the doctor to arrange a Medi-Vac as quickly as possible and specified that the aircraft fly at low attitude. Time was of the essence. The general showed up after I hung up. He was the one who gave my phone number to the doctor. He just said, "What do you need, Master Chief?"

"Sir, I need all that crap, including the chamber, off that tractor trailer now."

It's amazing how fast an entire base can work, when they know another service member is coming in on a life-and-death Medi-Vac. By the time we got the system off loaded and everything assembled, we could hear the chopper coming in. Unlike several weeks earlier, when we treated the staff sergeant, the weather was now hot and extremely humid, and that was going to be a problem.

When the physician brought her in, I asked him if she had any neurological symptoms. He said no, but from the way she was walking and speaking, I knew right away she was in dire need of help. I asked her how deep she had been diving and her voice was slurred. We loaded her up with a dive medic and pressed them both down to 165 feet.

Our environmental air conditioning package was not working, and the only way to cool the chamber was to vent it with our stored air. But the air compressor was not designed to keep up very long. The general showed up and asked how he could help. I told him I needed two things. His phone because mine won't make calls to America. I needed to talk to the Navy Experimental Diving Unit right away, and I needed ice, lots of ice. He gave me his phone and said that he would work on the ice, but there wasn't much ice in a desert.

I got the diving medical officer from the Navy Experimental Diving Unit on the phone within minutes, and told him about our patient, and what I'd done so far.

Meanwhile, my men were scrambling to connect a second air compressor, to continue venting the chamber to lower the temperature as best we could. It's amazing the amount of support you can leverage in these dire situations. Two helicopters arrived in just twenty minutes after my request for ice. The general and Marines came running in with body bags filled to the zippers with ice.

I asked where it came from and was told that the ice was flown from the aircraft carrier in the Battle Group. I locked one body bag full of ice into the outer lock and pressed it down to 165 feet. I then took two more and placed them on top of the chamber. The temperature began dropping immediately. The patient sat up and as I peered through the small window, she looked like a totally different person. Thankfully, she was responding to the treatment.

The diving medical officer suggested after her initial treatment, we follow up with five additional days of lengthy treatments in the chamber, and then stay on station for another 3 days afterward. However, our entire base was leaving the very next day. The general, upon hearing the necessary treatment, gathered the entire camp together and explained the situation. He asked for volunteers to stay behind for eight more days to help. Immediately, hands went up, and he had far more volunteers than needed. Every division left one or two marines behind, to support us in every way possible. The general left his chief of staff to ensure everything went smoothly.

After the camp departed, everyone moved into the pillbox with us, and someone remarked it was like a micro-command. But it was more like a big family, as all of us had the same mission, and that was to ensure our patient got better.

Eight days later we all went home.

Six months later, there was an all-hands ceremony on the base at Camp Lejeune. I absolutely hated these things. Every command on the base would have to stand in formation by command in a massive area the size of Tiananmen Square. I saw my buddy, the Base Sergeant Major, who was on the stage, tip his head toward me and give me a smile. When he stepped up to the microphone and said: "Oorah," all hands went still as a mouse. Everyone waited to hear what Sergeant Major had to say.

"It brings me great pleasure to invite my good friend, Master Chief Rick Bettua, to the stage, and the following Marines...." As myself and my Marines walked up to the stage, I noticed a woman in an Air Force dress uniform standing on stage, and it was the lieutenant from Turkey. They called my Marines up first, and the lieutenant awarded them all the Air Force Achievement Medal, for assisting with her recovery efforts.

Then I was called up, and my medal citation read for "directly saving her life." The lieutenant pinned the medal on me, then we both saluted each other. Next, we were supposed to shake hands, but she pushed my hand aside, wrapped her arms around me, and planted a big kiss on me in front of thousands of Marines.

In the background I could hear the general jokingly say, "Fucking sailors."

CHAPTER 19

DIVING IN 60 BELOW ZERO

One of the best things about being stationed on Camp LeJeune is that I could run every day for three years, and never take the same trail. By far, it was the best base I was ever stationed at for working out. One day after finishing a six-mile run, I came out of the woods near the dive locker, and saw a car parked out front with four stars on it.

I knew it could only be one person, and when I entered the building, the USMC commandant turned and asked, "How is my favorite Navy master diver doing today?"

"Sir, I'm the only master diver you know," I replied, and we shared a good laugh as we shook hands. I had met the commandant before, and was ready for his firm, slightly overzealous handshake that was accompanied with a toothy grin.

We sat down and he congratulated me and my dive team for our efforts in Turkey. Then he asked, "Does the Marine Corps possess the ability to dive in extreme cold water?"

I thought carefully about my answer, and then said, "No, the Marines are not trained for cold weather. I could provide the training, but we don't have the equipment."

"How much money do you need?"

"How many Marines would you like me to train, General?"

"You've already proven you can do a lot with eight men. So, eight, plus yourself, Master Chief."

I wanted to make sure I didn't cut myself short, so I answered, "Fifty grand, General."

He just laughed and said, "Make it happen."

I asked where the mission would be, and the commandant

said on the northern tip of Norway above the polar icecap. I suggested that we go somewhere cold prior to our trip, like Alaska, to acclimate ourselves.

We didn't have much time to get ready for our trip. All of us would need custom dry suits, as well as custom exposure suits. An exposure suit is just a lightweight dry suit, that keeps you dry and warm from the elements while you are working around the water, or in boats. We immediately ordered the cold-weather gear. We also ordered some cold water-approved diving equipment, specifically for scuba diving.

One of the most challenging aspects of preparing for this trip to the frigid north, was dealing with the Transportable Recompression Chamber. We had a new ten-foot by eight-foot shipping container with side doors, that I felt would work out perfectly. We mounted the inner lock of the chamber, and then bolted all the air flasks above it, to the overhead of the container. On the entrance side of the container, we ordered and installed a special round hatch, with a door the exact size as the chamber door, so we could load a patient and tender from the outside of the box. We also mounted an environmental package for hot and cold weather. Lastly, we had just enough room to pack two portable diesel-powered air compressors. The container was perfect. Our chamber was now in a single container ready to fly anywhere in the world.

We arrived in Seward Alaska in December of 1998, which just happened to be the coldest winter in the last twenty-five years. It was chosen for us because Seward is normally temperate, and the bay rarely ever freezes. That was not the case this particular year. When we arrived, we were looking at snow drifts over ten-feet high.

The marina was completely frozen.

Our host for the next several weeks was the Seward Chamber of Commerce. My point of contact was Theresa. Not much happens in Seward in the middle of winter. Fishing is shut down, and therefore all the canneries are closed. But that worked in our favor. Theresa found us an available cannery with a huge indoor bay. Upstairs there was a berthing facility for the fisherman. Besides beds, it included a living area with a TV, a nice commercial kitchen, showers, and of course lots of heat. The place was perfect for our needs.

It was important for us to spend as much time outdoors as possible, to get our bodies used to cold weather. Diving was important too, but to a lesser degree as the water temperature was almost ninety degrees warmer than the air. The air temperature upon our arrival was sixty degrees below zero Fahrenheit, and the water temperature was twenty-eight degrees.

The first day we decided to dive, we were faced with numerous challenges in the frigid temperatures, and our learning curve was very steep. I asked the harbor boat pilot to break up the ice in the marina, so we could dive within its confines before venturing out into the bay. We set up our gear inside the enclosed bay of the cannery, and once the boat captain called us, we all ventured outside.

The air temperature was enough to stop you dead in your tracks. It was painful to even take a breath. But we pushed on. Once at the marina, I had two marines dressed out in Drager and another marine dressed out in scuba, as the standby diver. In a matter of just ten minutes, the ice froze over again, and the divers were now standing on top of it, jumping up and down to break through.

The harbor boat was nearby, and the pilot readily agreed to make several more passes, to break up the ice once again. I could see the relief on the divers' faces as they finally immersed themselves in the icy water. It was a look of satisfaction because the water was so much warmer than the air. Once I turned their oxygen on and sent them on their way, the rest of the team and I needed to stay as warm as we possibly could. I had spared no expense outfitting all of us prior to our trip, with the very best extreme cold weather clothing money could buy. But with sixty below temperatures, it seemed like a feeble attempt. One of the things we learned that morning was to keep moving your feet, or they will freeze to whatever you are standing on.

Finally, the divers returned after a forty-minute dive, and we pulled them out of the water and into the freezing air. It took only seconds for the cold to turn them into ice colored sugar cookies. We stripped them out of the frozen dry suits, and into warm clothes. While urging everyone to hurry up on our way back to the cannery, I noticed a small coffee shop and I told everyone, "Let's go there. Coffee is on me."

As we entered the shop all dressed in solid black, everyone turned and looked at us. "Folks, if being a man in Alaska means you have to endure this type of weather, then I profess I am not a man," I said.

They all laughed, and the owner replied, "Son, we were just saying the same thing about all of you. We only go outside ten or fifteen minutes at a time. You've been out there for two hours."

The café and its patrons were extremely nice. They gave us a few pointers for staying warm, and introduced us to small chemical heating packs, called "toe warmers." They said they use them in their boots, gloves, and jackets. That day I went to every store in town, and purchased every case I could find, and put them on my government credit card.

Theresa at the Chamber of Commerce was really coming through for us. She called around town and got volunteers to invite us over for home-cooked meals. Every night each one of us was invited over to someone's house. Most of the volunteers were single women who had been cooped up too long in the dead of winter and were happy for the company and companionship.

The town also had a great bar, and every Friday and Saturday night a live band played. We soon discovered that every available girl in town would be at that same bar. We also discovered that fisherman didn't like to dance much, but we did. The girls outnumbered us four-to-one, and kept us busy until closing time, with one dance after another.

One night I remember going to the bar to get a drink, and I happened to bump into an extra-large human being who looked and smelled like a sasquatch. I politely said, "Excuse me." He turned around, obviously drunk and upset, and said "You better watch out little man. You could get hurt in here."

However, by the time he finished with his threat, at least four of my guys were standing right behind him, and Staff Sergeant Scott was not smiling. I said, "I think it's you who should be careful." With that, Scott and the boys threw him outside, and the bouncers thanked us for the help.

We were all having a great time in Seward. In doing so, we were inadvertently getting used to cold weather. One day after diving, Theresa called and asked if I could stop by her office. A good friend, Lieutenant Commander Chuck and I drove over to see her. Chuck was a Navy diving physician. He was with us in the event of an accident. He would also be going with us to Norway.

We walked into the warmth of the chamber of commerce, and Theresa met us both with a hot coffee, asked us how our stay was going, and if she could do anything more to help. We both laughed and asked how she could ever do more. We were all having a blast, and, by the way, we all loved the home cooked meals, I told her. With that, Theresa blushed a bit because she knew how our presence was helping the community. "Well, I think you boys are providing as much to us, as we are to you."

Then she said she wanted to ask us for a couple of favors. The first was that the owner of the cannery where we were living, wanted to know if we could check the outfall pipe from the cannery into the bay. It wouldn't affect our stay in the building, she said, if we couldn't do it.

When I asked her if she knew how deep the pipe was, she said about 150 feet and there was a buoy marking the end. I told her that Chuck and I would take care of it, that we were both Navy divers and qualified for much deeper dives. "What's the second thing?"

Theresa said she oversaw the annual March of Dimes event, and to raise money she wanted to auction my men and I for the charity. I asked her, what we would be responsible for doing. She said each of us would be going to dinner with the purchaser, and if anything transpired after dinner, that was between the two consenting adults.

"How can I say no to you?" I responded, and she said the event would be the coming Saturday night.

We were told to show up at the Lions Club at 9 p.m., but we weren't prepared for the magnitude of the event. There were hundreds of screaming women inside. When we walked in, many of them held wads of cash in their hands. Theresa met us and said the bar was open to us, but we could barely reach it since every girl in the place was trying to stake a claim.

There was one particular snow bunny who caught my eye, and she walked up to me and said, "You are as good as mine," and I replied, "I hope so."

My Marines and I each had a couple of drinks, and we walked around to mingle as much as we could. The auction started and all the Marines went from $400-$700. Surprisingly, the older you were, the more money you fetched. Next was our diving doctor Chuck, and Theresa, who was the auctioneer, really pushed the fact that he was a military doctor and was equipped to handle any broken heart. Chuck fetched the charity $1,200.

I don't know why Theresa kept me until last, but she was on stage building me up as the cream of the crop in her eyes. That's when an elderly woman walked in like she owned the place. My snow bunny and a few of her girlfriends occupied the front row, and the newly arrived woman sat way in the back. Theresa invited me to the stage, and once the bidding started the snow bunny stood up and screamed a bid of $1200. From the back of the room the elderly women trumped her by saying $1500. I had been bought by a woman twice my age. I took it in my stride and like a gentleman walked back to her to congratulate her. Then I asked what night she was free for dinner.

"Oh no, honey, you don't have to go to dinner with me. You go out with the other girl who was bidding on you with my blessing. I only do this each year to show these young bitches that I can."

I gave her a hug and a kiss on the cheek and said, "Thank you." I turned to see my snow bunny smiling and waiting for me. Like she had said when we first met earlier in the night. *You are as good as mine.* And I was.

Altogether, we raised almost $7,000 for the March of Dimes charity event.

It was a great way to say thank you to a town that was very good to us.

The big C-5 Galaxy Aircraft landed in Oslo Norway for Operation Battle Griffin on a beautiful crisp morning in 1999. To us, it felt like spring, although it was still minus 10 Fahrenheit.

As the other military personnel stepped off the plane, it was hilarious watching them trying to cope with the frigid cold, while we were all thankful for our time in Seward, Alaska.

It took us all day to reach our destination, which was above the Artic Circle, near the town of Tromso. The roads were ice packed, and the snow drifts were taller than our vehicles. We were headed to a small Marine camp near the entrance to the fjords. Once we arrived, I was greeted by the commanding officer, and executive officer of the USMC Riverine Assault Craft unit. They operated thirty-six-foot diesel-powered river patrol boats with massive jet drives along the fjords. They seemed somewhat surprised when our Force Recon dive team exited several Humvees, acting like they owned the place.

The executive officer, who was a major, asked if he could help us, and I replied, "Are you the commanding officer, sir?"

The commanding officer, a Lt. Colonel, replied, "I am, who the hell are you?"

"Hold on one second, sir, someone wants to speak to you."

I pulled my phone out and speed dialed my boss, the general, and he was on the phone before the second ring. "Did you make it, Master Chief?"

"Yes, sir, I did," I replied and told him the commanding officer wanted to know what we we're doing here."

"Let me speak to him."

I handed the phone over to the CO. It was a quick chat, but very cordial as I heard them both laughing on the line, and I heard the general say, "Take care of them."

The colonel hung up and looked at me and asked again, "Who the hell are you?"

I politely responded, "My name is Master Chief/Master Diver Bettua and I operate and train the Marine Corps Reconnaissance divers to handle water-borne missions."

The major then asked me, "What is a Master Chief?"

I laughed and said, "An incredibly young battalion sergeant major."

The colonel then asked, "Master Chief, may I ask what is your Chain of Command?"

I answered: "You sir, the Brigadier General you just spoke

to, and the Commandant of the Marine Corps." I could see the concern in his eyes and I said, "Colonel, we have several training missions scheduled with the Norwegian Special Forces, but when we are not operating with them, we will be glad to help out your unit in any way we can. I have some very senior Force Recon Marines that wouldn't mind training with your Marines and showing them a thing or two."

The major then said, "Master Chief, did you forget to add me to your chain of command?"

I replied, "No, sir, I didn't."

The following day we were invited to a "meet and greet" with the Norwegian team we would be working with. The meeting was to take place at 9 p.m. at a bar in town that was about twenty miles away. The Marines who worked with me were truly the very best set of professionals I'd ever worked with. Quiet, but very confident, they were all highly skilled in a variety of areas. I never had to worry about them and was genuinely proud to be in their company.

Although we drove our two military Humvees, we were all dressed in proper civilian clothes and arrived in town early. Just outside the bar in the center of town was a bronze statue of a family fleeing the bombs being dropped by Germany in the war, and I walked over to read about it. I was surprised to find out the town we were in, was completely destroyed during the war.

The bar was a big place with a massive fireplace roaring in the corner. By the time our drinks were served, the Norwegians arrived. There was no mistaking them when they walked in. They were ten of the largest men I'd ever seen. My Marines were not small men, but the Norwegians were clearly larger, and I was the runt in the litter. We all sat down with a drink and discussed the operation objectives, then by the second drink we were getting comfortable with each other. All the Norwegians spoke English well, which made things easy, and one soldier in particular spoke with no accent, and said he had gone to school in America.

He was the officer in charge of the unit, and the more he drank, the mouthier he became. He asked if U.S. forces were going to Bosnia, then made a comment to the effect that American soldiers ran around the world thinking they are some sort of police officers. I could feel my staff sergeant squeezing my thigh under the table without a smile on his face. In fact, no one was laughing, but the young officer. I tried my best to defuse the situation by saying, "We are just like you. We go where our government sends us."

The officer smugly responded, "But you stick your noses where they don't belong."

It was evident what was about to happen. None of my Marines were smiling, and each one was sizing up his opponent on the opposite side of the table. Finally, I said, "Well, I just found out this town was completely bombed by the Germans in the war, so it seems to me if we didn't stick our noses in your business, you would all be speaking fucking German right now!"

The table went flying. All the drinks hit the floor, and each one of my Marines had hold of a Norwegian before they could stand up. At that very moment, the young officer screamed to stop and apologized by saying, "You are right. I owe everyone a drink". I thought to myself, *Thank God. How would I ever explain a fight with the very people we are to train with?* We drank with them until midnight, and by the end of the night had grown respect for one another.

Although I can't talk about the operations we conducted during Battle Griffin, I did notice that all US special teams, such as, Force Recon, Navy SEALs, and Army Special Forces, are mostly comprised of alpha males. When our foreign services counterparts come and train with us, we always go first, and they follow our lead during any hazardous operation. The same was not true here. It was as if the Norwegians were unsure and reticent about their abilities. We would politely wait for them to go, only to receive a nod, for us to jump in front of them. It was as if their force had somehow lost their competitive edge—the alpha male spirit.

I remember thinking I hope we never lose that spirit in the U.S. armed forces. The military is not a democracy. It needs people willing to lead, and you cannot do that without taking that first step and leading from the front.

Our time in the Artic Circle was over, and we packed up our equipment to be transported to Oslo. With the equipment on the road, we only needed to grab our personal gear, weapons and say goodbye. At that very moment, a Marine ran into our tent and asked for me to follow him down to the pier. We walked down, and a few people were looking into the icy water, and I asked what was going on. A young lieutenant told me he was stepping over onto the pier from the boat, and he dropped an encrypted radio. I asked how much it cost, and he answered more than forty grand. But the more important thing, was that it was encrypted.

I hollered over to the boat driver and asked him the depth under his boat, and he answered, "Ninety-six feet, master chief." I asked my guys if anyone kept any diving gear, as ours was on the road to the airport. One of them said he had his mask, and I still had my exposure suit. I told my guys to go find two ammo cans and fill them with rocks. and bring at least one hundred feet of line.

I went back to my tent and donned my exposure suit. Hopefully, it would keep me warm enough for the short stint in the thirty-two-degree water. I walked back to the dock. I was not looking forward to getting in the icy water since I had no hood or gloves, just a mask and a thin exposure suit on. We tied the ammo cans together to the line, and I told my guys to hold them on the surface, and not to drop them until I gave a nod. I slipped into the water, and it felt like needles on my hands and face. I held onto the ammo cans as I tried to remove all the air from my exposure suit. Then I relaxed and started my three slow breaths.

Just when I was ready to go, a major ran up the pier yammering at us, demanded I get out of the water. I asked, "Who are you and why?"

He puffed his chest out, and exclaimed he was the safety officer, and what I was about to do was dangerous. I had already slowed my breathing down and was ready to descend despite his shouts.

"Marine, I order you to get out of the water now!"

I calmly replied, "I'm not a Marine," then nodded that I was ready. My Marines knew me well enough to know there was no way I was leaving an encrypted radio on the bottom in a foreign country. They released the heavy ammo cans, and I plummeted instantly toward the bottom. As the pressure squeezed on my exposure suit, I felt it pinching my skin. When I was halfway down, I spotted the radio. The ammo cans and I landed right next to it. For dark water the clarity was very good. I could see fish coming to check out the new visitor to the bottom, and a curious crab clamped down on the radio as if to claim it. Although the radio was much larger than he was, he looked determined to take it home.

The bottom was quiet, so I took an extra minute to remind myself why I enjoyed free diving so much, while soaking up the serenity before finally grabbing the radio. I let go of the ammo cans and skyrocketed back to the surface. Now the major was red-faced and screaming that he was going to put me and my Marines on report. The Riverine Commanding Officer showed up and told the safety officer to calm down, but the major demanded to know my rank and who I worked for.

The CO put his arm around his shoulders, and while walking away said, "You don't want to know."

CHAPTER 20

BLOW IT IN PLACE

The more senior I became, the less fun I was having. By 2007, my diving days were long over and now the sailors who once worked for me had become master divers as well. My last command in the Navy was Mobile Diving Salvage Unit One in Pearl Harbor Hawaii, where I was billeted as the command master chief. Mobile Diving Salvage Unit-1 is the largest operational diving command in the world. It is responsible for diving operations from California to the Middle East. It is comprised of eight independent dive teams, and each has its own master diver.

As the command master chief, my job was to fix problems in every facet of our day-to-day operations and personnel management, and that included discipline. My title was a high honor for my decades of service. It also brought home the reality that increasingly my job was to deal with bad situations. Some were heart-breaking, and I personally felt the emotional traumas.

Sailors might think they know the duties of the command master chief, but they are usually wrong. My definition would startle most sailors. I worked for the commanding officer by representing the crew, but most importantly my job was to ensure we didn't fail as a command. By that time in my career, leadership was easy, I had been a master chief for more than fourteen years, and a master diver even longer. Many of the sailors in the crew had worked for me at previous commands, and that was a testament that I was doing my job well.

During my final four years, my job was demanding because

it wasn't my nature to sit back and not to participate in the diving tasks. I was involved with everything from training, operations, discipline, and even family advocacy. The most difficult aspect of my job was working with family advocacy, which dealt with physical, mental, and sexual abuse issues inside the homes of my sailors.

You step into a job like this with the best intentions, only to discover the world can be a very dark place. It was dealing with these dark issues that took the biggest toll on me. Leadership schools teach us to treat everyone equally, but with years of seniority under my belt, I realized that wasn't possible. A poor leader will always try to appease everyone, while a good leader will make unpopular decisions and stand by his convictions, because they are the right thing to do. I can honestly say that I did a good job, but the stress it caused was enormous, and my commanding officer could see it.

About six months before my retirement, he came into my office and said I was going on a job. I just shook my head and said, "Sir, you know I don't go on any jobs." He replied that this job was for both me and my wife, Angela, as a sort of thank you for years of dedicated service to the command.

When I asked him to tell me more, he said, "You and Angela are going to the island of Palau for three weeks, and your only job is to babysit two marine biologists doing a reef survey. Make sure you pack a speargun, Master Chief."

The commanding officer also didn't want me to worry about a thing, so he decided to send a warrant officer named Christopher, who would handle all the logistics. Christopher and I had been close friends for over ten years, and he, too, was a master diver, who later in his career shifted over to become a warrant officer. When we first met, we were like oil and water, but then we realized that we both liked boats and fishing, and that was our common ground.

Palau is an archipelago and part of Micronesia, a beautiful island with a fringing reef and a deep-water port. A U.S. Navy ship was pulling into the port when the Palauan pilot struck a reef during a violent rainstorm. Micronesia then requested four million dollars from the U.S. government because 100 square yards of reef was destroyed, even though their own pilot was in charge of the ship at that time.

Angela and I, along with Christopher, flew to Guam, then to the island of Yap en route to Palau. Yap was just a stopover, but peering down at the island from the plane, it looked like spearfishing heaven, and I commented to Angela that we should go there someday.

The plane landed in Palau and a good friend of mine, Henni, picked us up and drove us to the resort hotel. Henni, who was from South Africa, was one of the best spearfishermen I knew. I had spearfished with him in the South Pacific, and I am the godfather of his son, Taei. He lived on Palau, and since he had a new twenty-seven-foot boat, I asked him if he wanted to work for the U.S. Navy for the next three weeks. He said that would be great because business was slow. I told him we needed him and his boat and asked how much per day. He answered, "Just $100 a day because we are friends."

Christopher and I looked at each other and I said, "We can't pay you $100 per day. How about $500 per day, all inclusive— fuel, oil, lunch and drinks for everyone?"

"Are you kidding?" he responded.

"No mate, not kidding, $500 a day."

This might seem like a lot of money, but our mission was to investigate a claim of $4 million dollars of damaged reef.

Even though 600,000 people are in the U.S. Navy, there were only two civilian marine biologists. Later that evening, we met them for drinks and dinner. We spoke about the jobsite, which was about twenty-five miles away inside the reef, and Henni said he knew the spot well.

I asked them both how much time per day they needed to be on location. We had a total of twenty-one days to complete this task. The senior biologist said that he'd know more once we visited the job site. During dinner the two marine biologists seemed to have some pre-conceived notion that Christopher and I had been sent out to Palau to support them, and at the first mention suggesting we were working for them, Christopher glanced over at me. It took me a second or two longer to digest what the biologist had just said. They expected us to charge their scuba cylinders every day.

I replied, "Stop right there. I think you are confused. We are the US Navy, and we have been sent to ensure you complete the job without getting hurt. You will do what I say, when I say it, or I'll put your asses back on the plane tonight, understood?"

They both nodded in agreement. Then I explained: "Gentlemen, this is my last job after thirty years of service, and I have every intention of having as much fun as possible with or without you. Christopher and I have almost sixty years of diving experience between us. I am sure we can measure a damaged reef."

The table was uncomfortably quiet for a few moments, so Angela stood up and made a toast. "Here's to Rick's last official Navy dive job."

The following morning, we loaded up and headed out to the damaged reef. Palau is spectacular with high lush mountains and crystal-clear blue water, and as Henni's boat cruised over reefs, we could see all the colorful coral below. It took us almost an hour to get to the spot. The inner reef was flat like a mirror when we arrived, and we could clearly see the damage to the reef thirty feet down. However, we soon realized the damage was nowhere as large as what was reported.

I suggested before the biologist dove in scuba, that we all snorkel around the area to get a good understanding of the size. The moment we hit the water, we saw that the entire damaged area was only about ten square yards, one-tenth of what the Micronesian government was claiming. We all got back in the boat, and got our scientist prepared to dive.

Although the area was small, they needed to mark it out, and take a comprehensive set of photos. An hour later, the biologist returned to the boat, and we all sat down for a talk. I asked them what they needed, and the senior biologist said they only needed twenty hours to complete the job. I told them that this type of job has only come up once in my thirty-year career, and Christopher, Angela, and I weren't going home early.

They explained they didn't want to go home early, either, and that they both were avid underwater photographers. I asked again, "What do you want?" They said they only wanted to visit the site one hour per day, and if possible, after that they wanted us to take them out to the drop off so they could take photos the rest of the day. I replied, "Only if I get to spearfish." With that, we struck an accord with the two marine biologists and everyone was happy.

The top of the reef had a consistent depth of fifty to sixty feet, then it dropped down to several thousand feet. Not only was the coral in pristine shape, but large predators like sailfish, Spanish mackerel, and dogtooth tuna cruised along the drop off in search of a meal.

I would employ a flasher, which is nothing more than several mirrors attached to a floating line, that would dangle down about seventy-five feet. The predators would see it, then come up from the depths to investigate, allowing me to shoot them. Very few fish in the world can match a dogtooth tuna's power. They are notorious dirty fighters, running straight for the reef, and attempt to try to dislodge the spear or cut the line. These tunas are often in the company of large sharks, and no shark loves them more than the Pacific silver fringe.

The silver fringe is not a well-known shark, but it can always strike fear in me. It's large and very fast and will pounce on a dogtooth tuna in a second. One day after the biologists were finished diving, Henni said he knew an amazing spearfishing spot that may have some dogtooth. The spot was on a long stretch of reef near a corner and the drop off was very steep. This caused a massive upwelling of turbulence and nutrients that brought in baitfish.

Christopher, Henni, and I got in the water, which was alive with rainbow runners (baitfish), and we could see at least twenty sharks, half of them silver fringe. You need two things to find dogtooth tuna: rainbow runners and silver fringe sharks. Find them both together, and dogtooth tuna will likely be close by.

I lowered the flasher down to seventy-five feet, and instinctively the sharks swarmed it. They were circling it, then bumping it to see if it was edible. But after about fifteen minutes, most of them lost interest. I asked Christopher if he wouldn't mind being "flasherman," and told him to slowly yank on the mirrors to mimic wounded baitfish. Another fifteen minutes passed, I wasn't paying attention but then I heard Christopher yelling. I swam over to him, and he pointed down toward the flasher. He said he saw something silver down there, and I replied. "Yeah, three or four big silver fringe sharks.

He said no, it was something else, so I told him I would take a look. I took my usual three deep breaths and made my dive, sliding down seventy-five feet while holding my breath. I counted three silver fringe sharks, and I looked over to see a large dogtooth tuna swimming slowly away.

I kicked toward it, and when I was at about ninety feet, the tuna turned to look at me. Instinctively, I fired the speargun and the shaft hit it just behind its head. The moment that gun went off, ten silver fringe sharks showed up for the feast. As I swam for the surface, some of them chased the dogtooth and others followed me. I broke the surface and shouted for Christopher to get in the boat. The last thing I saw was a half a dozen silver fringe sharks closing in on my prize. I jumped into the boat and told Christopher to pull the line as hard as he could, and together we kept it away from the frenzy of ravenous sharks. It was my first dogtooth, and it tipped the scales at 101 lbs.

Near the end of the job, the two marine biologists faxed their report to the Navy legal department that was handling the case. A short time later, the senior marine biologist received a call from a Navy lawyer. They discussed a few things, and then the lawyer asked to speak to me. He said he was prior enlisted and wanted to get my take on the damage.

"The marine biologist report is correct," I said, "and the area of concern is only a tenth of what was claimed. Therefore, my suggestion is to pay them one-tenth of the amount they are seeking."

The Micronesian government received $400,000 for the grounding incident, and my spearfishing holiday saved American taxpayers 3.6 million dollars.

Just a few months prior to my retirement, I was visited by an old shipmate Captain Mark. He was retired from the Navy, and now an administrator with the Military Sealift Command

(MSC), an organization made up of government service employees and contractors that controls U.S. Navy transport ships. At lunch, he told me he was creating two positions for master divers, one in the Atlantic, the other in the Pacific. The job title was diving, salvage and towing advisor, and he was offering me the position for the Pacific. I asked him who the other master diver was, whom he was considering for the Atlantic position. It was a good friend who I very much respected: Eric.

I told him I was planning on living in Kona, Hawaii after my retirement and he said that was fine, I didn't need to report to an office. Everything sounded great, and I accepted the position.

When Captain Mark asked me to sign a contract, I asked him why that was necessary, that I was happy to take on the job. He replied, "Because we don't want you working for someone else." I signed the contract and told him I was taking terminal leave the following week. Terminal leave can be taken at the end of one's career for a maximum time of ninety days with pay.

The captain was pleased. "Great, I have your first job for you. Do you know where the island of Yap is?"

I started laughing and told him I was just there. The job was an easy one that entailed only me flying to Yap and taking soundings at various points inside the harbor basin. I was told an MSC ship was going to be coming in for a port o' call, but satellite images appeared to show that the basin looked too shallow for the ship. The Navy wanted to confirm that it was deep enough.

Only two flights a week flew in and out of Yap, so I was planning on being there for one week to complete the soundings. Then, if time allowed, I would get in some spearfishing too. I arrived in Yap, and once I checked into the Manta Ray Hotel, I asked the owner if he could arrange a boat and boat driver for me for at least the next five days. Being a boat enthusiast prior to leaving Hawaii, I put together a portable depth sounder with a built-in GPS chart plotter and mounted it all inside a waterproof pelican case. The system even had a rechargeable lithium battery that would last all day. It would make things easy for me, as I could check the depth and mark the GPS position if any anomalies existed.

The following morning after breakfast, I departed with my new Yap friend, Albert, my boat driver. We needed to take over one hundred depth soundings, and record each during high tide, then again at low tide. Albert also had a new depth sounder on his boat making it that much easier. Between us, we completed the task easily in one day. Being as it was my first job working for MSC, I couldn't afford to make any mistakes. So the following day, Albert and I went back into the basin to check all the marks again at both high and low tide.

Late in the afternoon back at the hotel, the owner saw me looking at a chart of the island and asked if he could help. I asked him where on the chart would I find the most sharks. He pointed to the north end of the reef, and said it was out of control up there, but I couldn't go. I asked him why, and he said I would need the chief's permission and he has never let anyone dive that point for safety reasons.

In Polynesian culture, the chief and tribe that own the land also own the water that is extended from it. The owner of the hotel knew the chief and he brought me to him. After a bit of pleading with the chief, he finally said I could visit the northern end, but only if I took both of his sons with me. They were in their twenties but had never been to the sharky north end of the reef.

Polynesian stories are passed down through generations. Even the chief himself had not been there, but he wanted to know if the stories were true. The following day, I ventured to the north end of the reef, accompanied by the chief's two sons. The water was crystal clear, and you could see the reef seventy feet below, and beyond it, the wall of deep dark blue. We stayed right on the edge of the reef, with the deep blue to our left, the reef to our right, and finally I killed the engine.

One of the chief's sons had been looking forward to jumping in with me prior to arriving. But the moment the boat stopped, it was surrounded by sharks, and he said, "No way!" I slipped into the clear water by myself, and it seemed the stories were true. At least a hundred sharks were swimming around me.

I could tell these sharks had never seen a human being. They were curious, but not aggressive.

However, as I looked down, I could see several huge dogtooth tuna, some over two hundred pounds and six feet long. They were swimming slowly in the current under the watchful eyes of an army of sharks. There would be no way for me to land one, even if I could shoot it, but I planned to come back in the future with more divers to watch my back.

My job in Yap was done and the following day I was scheduled to fly home. That evening while having a drink in the hotel bar, a hippie-looking guy walked up to me and asked me if I was a Navy diver. I replied yes, and he told me he was a marine biologist from the States doing research. I asked how I could help him, and he said, "I think I found a mine." I asked him where, and he said in the middle of the channel, at a depth of about 115 feet.

I grabbed a pen from the bartender and gave him a napkin and asked him to draw what he had seen. His drawing was good enough to cause concern. I asked if he would show me where it was, and he said absolutely not. He didn't ever want to go near it again.

The bar where we were sitting was elevated, and you could see the basin and the entrance to the channel. I asked him to point to where he saw the mine, and his finger was aimed at the center of the channel. The following day, I went out with Albert again and brought along scuba gear. The tide was ebbing, and my plan was to just go down and drift with the outgoing tide to see if I could locate it.

Many people will tell you never to dive alone, and for good reason, but in the Navy we work underwater by ourselves all the time, and it was second nature to me. I asked Albert to follow my bubbles and told him I would be staying on the left side of the channel but flowing toward the sea. I also towed a small buoy so he could see me more easily on the surface, and I could mark the mine. The water in the basin was relatively clear. I could still see about fifty feet.

My plan was to try to stay at one hundred feet and keep looking. I hopped into the water and gave Albert a smile and an okay, then started swimming down. I couldn't see the bottom until I got to about sixty feet. I continued down to one hundred feet and just floated with the current like a piece of seaweed.

I looked up and down along the edge of the channel as fast as I could. The current had picked up and I was moving much faster than when I got in. The biologist said it was on the left side of the channel. But if it wasn't there, I was prepared to dive the right side as well. The channel up ahead bent sharply to the left, and I couldn't see what was on the opposite side. When I came around the corner it was right in front of me.

Seeing a five-hundred-pound mine in a book is a lot different than running into one underwater. I ascended to ninety feet and had a good look. It was not of a type I had seen before, and it looked brand new. I thought it to be odd that no growth at all was present on the mine. I tied my float line to a coral head to mark the mine, and then ascended.

As soon as I got back to the hotel, I called Capt. Mark and explained the situation. He asked for the phone number of the hotel and told me to stand by. I would receive a call shortly. Only minutes went by when the phone rang, and I was greeted by the commodore of the Explosive Ordnance Disposal Group 1, who was actually MDSU-1's commodore. He said, "Master Chief Bettua, how are you?"

I corrected him by saying, "It's just Rick now, Commodore. I am on terminal leave."

"Good for you, Rick. Now tell me what you have."

I explained that there was a five hundred-pound mine in the center of the channel going into Yap, and an MSC ship was scheduled to arrive in a few weeks for a port o' call. He told me to standby, and shortly a lieutenant picked up and asked me to describe the mine. I told him the mine's unique characteristics and he asked how close I'd gotten to it.

"About ten feet from it," I told him.

"Good thing you didn't touch it. It's the most dangerous type."

Explosive Ordnance Group 1 scrambled a dive team out of Guam with a Navy C-130 aircraft. They would place charges near the mine and blow it in place. The U.S. government spends an ungodly amount of money on training sailors in all special teams. The risk of losing divers by attempting to disarm a mine, is much greater than simply placing a very inexpensive charge next to it, getting a safe distance away, and then detonating it, and the mine, in a controlled explosion. The procedure is called BIP–Blow it in Place.

CHAPTER 21

FINAL DIVE

As the plane approached Saipan in the Marietta Islands in December of 2009, I marveled at the island's geography—rugged cliffs on one side, sandy beaches on the other, and crystal-clear water and reefs surrounding the island. This would be a very quick trip to give me an understanding as to the magnitude of an upcoming job. We needed to clear the main channel of coral heads (reef), which had grown since the channel was initially dredged some fifty years earlier.

When I arrived, the Port of Saipan manager explained to me that unless the coral reefs were removed from the channel, larger ships, including U.S. Naval vessels and cruise ships, soon would not be able to enter the port. That would put a serious financial strain on the local economy, which relied on port traffic. The main area of concern was approximately one hundred yards wide, and five hundred yards long. A Navy side-scan sonar team was mapping out every obstacle in the channel, which was shallower than fifty feet below the surface. Our job would be to remove it.

The following day I met up with the sonar techs from the side-scan team, introduced myself, and asked if I could tag along. The lieutenant in charge had been told I would be showing up. She asked how she could help, and I asked her to take me to the twenty highest points that they had already mapped.

She replied, "Only twenty?" I asked how many there were, and she said at least sixty.

I had my free diving gear with me and was over the side in a flash once the boat stopped on the first mark. The sonar technicians didn't know what to think. I was just gone, and they watched me as I swam to the bottom. The water was crystal clear and I noticed it was a coral head that had grown and resembled a stalk of broccoli. The base of the coral was approximately six feet in diameter, but the head was the size of a small car. I returned to the surface and jumped back in the boat.

People who are not accustomed to seeing free divers always ask the same question, and the lieutenant and her team were no exception. "That was incredible, how long can you hold your breath for?"

I don't think I have ever truly answered that question. I just explain that I have been doing it my whole life. It took me the better part of the morning to dive on the remaining coral heads before I was satisfied and knew I could come up with a plan to remove them.

The USS *Salvor* ARS-52, now operated by Military Sealift Command, and a dive team from my former command Mobile Diving Salvage Unit 1, were not scheduled to arrive in Saipan for several weeks for the job. That gave me time to ensure everything needed was onboard *Salvor* prior to her leaving Pearl Harbor. The following day I jetted back to Kona, Hawaii to prepare for the upcoming trip.

At 5 a.m. my phone rang. *I thought to myself you got to be kidding me. I didn't even get home until midnight.* I tried to focus my blurry eyes and saw that the phone said, Captain Mark "Boss." I answered with a very tired, "Good morning, Boss."

Captain Mark asked when I had gotten home and after I told him just five hours ago, he asked me how fast I could get to Pearl Harbor Shipyard Conference Center? I told him that I would need to catch a flight, but at this hour it was no problem. "I can be there by 10 a.m."

"Get there as soon as you can and help them with the problem we've got." He added that he was flying to Vietnam and wouldn't be available for the next week. Before I could ask what the problem was, he hung up.

Angela sat up, looked at me, and said, "Really, you just got home? I think you travel more now than when you were on active duty." I knew she was right, and promised to make it up to her, then headed back to the airport.

I was escorted into the conference center, which looked like sheer chaos when I looked in through the window. There were more than fifty people in the room, and most of them were trying to talk over one another. I paused outside the door and glanced at my escort. Was this really the right conference room? "Are you sure?"

He said yes and opened the door. I had absolutely no idea why I was there, and then, over all the noise, I heard a familiar voice. It was the ship's harbor pilot Mike telling everyone to settle down, and that I was the person he was talking about. A man stepped out of the crowd, approached me, and introduced himself as a producer working for Universal Pictures.

"I have several questions for you. Do you possess the Navy Qualification 5341, Master Diver?"

After I said I did, he asked how long I'd been a master diver, and I told him about twenty years. Still not knowing what this was all about, the producer then asked me if I could rig the battleship USS *Missouri* for tow in eight days.

I took my time to reply. The USS *Missouri* is the 45,000-ton battleship where Japan surrendered at the end of World War II, and it was now a floating museum. "I guess I can do anything in eight days with the right amount of logistical support."

I told him that we would need some unique equipment that was extremely heavy, and it was located in Seattle. I added that I would also need a crew to help me rig the ship. The producer, who seemed desperate, then quickly asked if I knew how to rig it.

"Yes, of course."

My response seemed to upset people in the room. The producer turned to the Pearl Harbor Shipyard CEO and said, "How is it that he can do the job in eight days, but you want me to employ your shipyard for four weeks? I guess my problem is you, you're fired!"

With that, ninety percent of the people in the room walked out. The producer then introduced me to his staff, and we all sat down. He asked me about the equipment we needed. I explained that every piece of rigging would need to be certified, and the only place which would have it on short notice, was in Seattle. I had the business listed on my phone and called them immediately. I asked if they had the following items in stock and certified—four shots of three-inch chain (one shot equals ninety feet), two three-inch anchor shackles, and four detachable shackles for the three-inch chain.

The owner of the business confirmed everything was in stock, and certified. Then he said it would take five pallet loads, and the total weight would be 34,000 pounds. After getting off the phone, I explained the equipment was in stock, but the biggest obstacle was getting the equipment to Hawaii. The producer responded that would be no problem because Universal owned a cargo plane. Just like that the equipment was ordered and would be delivered to the airport the following day.

The producer then said, "What else do you need, Master Diver?"

I told him I would need the best set of riggers in the world, and they were either here in Hawaii doing a job, or back in Samoa. Before that meeting was, over someone from the team called out, "They are in Samoa, but when they heard your name, they said they were coming."

I then asked the producer why he was so adamant that I was a qualified 5341? He said it was related to insurance for moving the famous nine-hundred-foot museum out to sea. Lloyds and Lloyds of London was charging a million dollars for the twelve-hour task. "The stipulation was that we needed someone with your qualifications onboard, to oversee the operation."

Two days later, I heard the Samoan riggers long before I could see them, giving the security team a hard time on the quarterdeck of the *Missouri*. When I walked around the corner, all eight of them shouted, "Unko Rick," and I told the security team they were with me.

Then came the painful task of saying hello to a bunch of overstuffed giant teddy bears, who weighed 300-425 pound each. I thought they were going to break my ribs. I met Aiga Riggers down in Samoa while doing a job removing 86,000 gallons of Aviation Fuel on a sunken wreck in the harbor. Samoans love life, and they especially love eating fish. While in Samoa, I went spearfishing on weekends and would give whatever I caught to their families, and before I knew it, I was family too.

When it came to moving heavy items and working hard, these guys never got tired, and they never complained. Aleki, the oldest in the family, was the boss. He asked, "What we need to do, Unko?" I pointed to the five pallets of gear on the pier, and told him that when he was ready, all that needed to be brought aboard.

It was midnight before the crew was ready to bring the gear aboard, and that's when my phone rang. It was an unregistered number and when I answered, Capt. Mark's boss introduced himself, and then asked me what I was doing?

"Rigging the USS *Missouri* to be towed as per Capt. Marks orders."

"Master Diver, I want you to stop and walk off the job right now."

"Sir, I can't do that. I have already given my word to rig and tow this ship."

He again demanded that I walk off or he would fire me. "No sir, I won't do that. I was allowed to retire onboard the USS *Missouri*, and I won't walk away from her."

Then I hung up on him. Aleki came over and asked if I was okay, and I told him I was probably going to get fired because of some stupid political battle. Then he asked, "We finish the job, Unko?"

"Yes, Aleki. We always finish the job." My phone rang several times, but from the same number. I ignored the calls. Then it rang from my Atlantic counterpart, Eric, and he asked what was going on. I told him I was rigging the *Missouri* for tow, and he replied, "Holy shit, I would give my right arm to be on that job."

It would be the pinnacle of any master diver's career to tow the USS *Missouri*, and I was not going to walk away. But apparently Eric knew the consequences. "I admire you, Rick, but you are going to get fired if you don't walk away from it."

"I can't do that, Eric. I gave them my word."

"I don't blame you one bit. I wouldn't walk either."

By this point in my career, I had been around long enough to know it was all about a political blame game. Military Sealift

Command (MSC) did not want to take on the responsibility of an accident, which if it occurred would become international news. Even though I worked through a separate sub-contractor, MSC still paid my salary, and in the event of an accident, the paper trail would lead back to them. The risk was not worth the reward.

If they fired me before the tow, they could feel justified in saying I was working as an independent contractor. A few days later the most beautiful day in Hawaii, a trans-Pacific tug from the West Coast showed up to tow the massive battleship. I was on the forecastle (bow) of the *Missouri* working with the tug crew, before finally releasing the chain, and then coordinating the ship's movements. The operation went absolutely flawlessly and the *Missouri* was filmed at sea from every conceivable angle by helicopters, planes, and wave piercing boats.

It takes about sixty sailors to get a battleship underway even if it is at tow. Countless numbers of lines connected from the pier to the ship, must be manhandled. Young sailors from Pearl Harbor volunteered to be a part of getting the battleship underway, for the Universal Pictures movie, *Battleship.* All of them stayed out of sight of the cameras at sea, by sitting under the forward eighteen-inch gun mounts that were on the forecastle.

I got the opportunity to meet them all and was having fun answering all the questions they could conger up. It was about noon when the assistant producer came to the forecastle and asked if I would join them for lunch. I was looking forward to it because I heard one of Honolulu's best restaurants was doing all the catering. But as we were walking by the gun mounts, I asked the sailors underneath if they had already eaten. I was told no and asked the assistant producer what the plan for them was.

She said the production staff completely overlooked them. I explained to her that I couldn't eat either. As we were discussing the situation, the producer showed up and asked, "Master Diver, you are joining us for lunch, yes?"

I politely said, "No, sir, I can't. You see in the military, senior people always eat last to ensure there is enough food for the crew. I would rather politely decline than to enjoy a meal knowing these kids have not been fed."

The producer looked at his assistant and said, "Make it happen." Then he added, "We will all wait." Less than an hour later, you could hear the chopper overhead as they lowered down sixty quality lunches for all the sailors onboard.

The operation was a success, and now the USS *Missouri* was back at her normal birth at the museum. I said goodbye to the producer and the production team and stepped off the USS *Missouri* for the last time. As I was walking to my rental car, my phone rang, and it was Capt. Mark. His extra loud gregarious voice bellowed, "Great job, Master Diver."

I replied, "Am I fired, Boss?"

"No, you're not fired. In fact, just the opposite. There will be a little something extra in your next paycheck from the folks that threatened to fire you. Get some rest and spend some time with your Aussie Queen. I'll see you in Saipan next week."

I came awake the moment the jet touched down on the island of Guam. I had a good sleep courtesy of my travel agent, Edna, who was a wonderful lady living in a Colorado retirement village. She knew where I wanted to sit on the plane, down to the very seat, and she always had me in economy-plus or business class. Most importantly, Edna worked for me twenty-four hours a day, and she never minded me waking her up from the opposite side of the world. I admired the fact that although Edna was retired, she still wanted to stay busy, and so she supported me and a few other ex-military contractors that needed instant travel plans, on a moment's notice.

Her fee for services was ten percent, but she was worth every dime. I cannot count how many times she got me out of a jam and redirected me to a new destination. Edna was the type of person who loved her job, and in doing so, she made me look extraordinary.

As I walked to my next gate for the plane going to Saipan, I turned my phone on. The first thing that popped up was a message from Captain Mark. "Going to be a couple of days late. Represent us well and look out for our best interest during the in-brief."

I texted back, "I always do."

The flight to Saipan, which is in the northern Marianas Islands, from Guam was a short hop. Once I arrived, I needed to get over to the USS *Salvor* and speak to the captain and the master diver as quickly as possible, before the in-brief started. As I pulled up to the pier and got out of my rental car, I noticed the *Salvor* was just pulling in.

I gave a wave to Captain Ed who was on the bridge maneuvering and calling out for which lines to put out. Then I walked toward the fantail because I saw something that wasn't right. In fact, it was downright dangerous. Two young divers were sitting up on the cap rail, while the ship was maneuvering both engines to get closer to the pier. If one of them fell into the water, he would be killed by the ship's propellers.

I've noticed that leaders nowadays don't want to be the bad guy and are very restrained about telling subordinates not to do something, or even demand that they act quickly. But I didn't grow up in that generation. I yelled, "Get the fuck off that cap rail now!" Startled, they both jumped to their feet and gave me a look that said, *Who the hell are you?* Then they retreated to the dive locker.

They must've gone inside and told their master diver that a civilian on the pier just yelled at them, and to rally some support. Sure enough, the entire dive team filed out with master diver Paul in the lead to confront me. As soon as Paul recognized me, he gave me a big smile and said, "Hello, Master Chief." Paul explained to his team, "That is Master Chief/Master Diver Bettua. He was my master diver just like I am yours. You will do what he says without hesitation. One more thing, when you speak to him, you will address him as master chief and I better not hear any of you call him Rick."

Paul was a good friend, and I was glad he was on this job. He had worked for me several times during my career and I remember the day when he walked into my office and asked me how to become a chief petty officer. I asked him if he was sure, and he said that he was.

"This will hurt me more than you, as I hate to lose you". I had sat on my fair share of Chief, Senior Chief, and Master Chief boards during my career, and I knew from real experience what would get him to the top the fastest. "I am going to terminate your shore duty, and have you transferred to the USS *Salvor*. I want you to run the deck department and to qualify as officer of the deck as quickly as you can. If you do that, you will be advanced the first time up." Paul was smart and very driven. He did just what I told him and made chief at the first opportunity. Then when he left *Salvor*, he became a master diver.

Captain Ed waved me onboard, and I told Paul to tag along so we could have a talk before the meeting. Paul had no idea I had been to Saipan to do a pre-inspection. I explained to both Paul and Captain Ed, that I wanted to remain quiet at the meeting, and only get involved if a serious matter presented itself. Then I told Paul that I wanted him to promote my dive plan, which was nothing more than moving the ship into a two-point moor, then using 1-1/4 inch wire rope to choke the base of the coral heads with the ship's capstan– a vertical-axled rotating device that multiplies the pulling force when hauling ropes or cables . If the capstan could not break them free, then the ship's buoyancy would certainly do the trick, using the ocean swells.

I also said there is a good chance Mariana's Environmental Agency will be in the room. "If they ask you the impact of killing the coral, I want you to say that we are not killing the coral, we are relocating them each day. You see, coral is made up of billions upon billions of individual cells and breaking the base off won't kill the coral."

I asked Captain Ed if he had any concerns and he explained that he wanted his ship to stay pier side and not go out to an anchorage. I asked why, and he said that Saipan's Lighterage (anchoring) Services cost $8,000 per day, and I knew his ship was slated to be here for several weeks.

The meeting started at 1 pm. in the conference room of the Harbor Control Building, and the room was packed with people from different agencies from around the island. Also in the group was the Saipan governor, the mayor, and the harbor master. The meeting started with refreshments, and small talk, and everyone in the room thanked us for coming to help clear the channel's entrance.

Master Diver Paul started off by explaining the game plan for the operation. I have to say he did a better job than I could've done. Before the environmental team could object, Paul beat them to the punch line, exclaiming that the operation had the environment at the top of its priority list, and how he planned on relocating the coral without killing it. Everyone seemed pleased, all nodding in agreement with smiles on their faces.

When Captain Ed expressed an interest in the *Salvor* returning pier side every evening after operations were done for the day, he was immediately shut down. The Harbor Master exclaimed *Salvor* was to go to anchorage daily. The room fell silent, and I could see the disappointment on Ed's face. I spoke up and said, "No!" The governor, mayor and harbor master all looked at me and I added: "Absolutely not!"

The governor asked who I was, and I replied, "My name is Rick Bettua. I represent the US Navy and MSC. Respectfully, there is no way we are coming here to help you with your situation and pay you $8,000 per day to stay at anchor. So, either you wave the lighterage fee for the anchorage, or you allow *Salvor* to tie up pier side every day for free. If that is not acceptable with you, the ship will get underway back to Hawaii tomorrow morning." Captain Ed's eyes went wide as he knew I did not have the power to cancel the operation and order the ship home to Hawaii, but he sat silently and waited for an answer.

Although the harbor master was red faced and upset that he was losing what would have been well over $150,000 in harbor revenue, the governor said, "I'm sure we can accommodate that, Rick. *Salvor* can come back to the pier each day." With that, the meeting was over.

The job itself was a very easy task for Paul and his team onboard *Salvor*. Each day we would go to sea, drop several anchors at a new location, and harvest the coral heads. We would then relocate the coral heads to the deep side of the reef. In total, we cleared more than seventy of them. I sat up on the boat deck near the king post in a comfortable chair watching the team dive and found myself daydreaming and wondering where the last thirty years had gone. It seemed to me that in the blink of an eye, I was transformed from a young kid determined to get to dive school, to the very epitome of the first master diver I met at the Pentagon three decades ago.

The daydream was cut short when I heard Paul shout up to me. "Hey, Master Chief, you wanna dive?"

It was something I thought I would never hear again. "You don't have to ask me twice," I responded and raced down to the dive station. Paul was taking a huge risk offering me a dive. After all, I was a civilian and no longer in the Navy. If something were to go wrong, it would be shouldered by him alone, and more than likely it would be the end of his very promising career.

But really what could possibly go wrong? It was a beautiful day, crystal clear water that was only fifty feet deep. I put on heavy boots and an MK-21 hardhat. My dive partner was fresh out of second-class dive school and smiled from ear to ear when I pointed to him and said, "I am red diver and young man, you are green diver." Once we were hatted up, and our communication checks completed, we each stood up, moved to the edge of the ship, and then jumped into the water.

As we slid down the descent line, I was already looking at a coral head which I hadn't seen on my initial inspection. At first it appeared not to have a stalk to choke off, as if the head itself was attached to the bottom. How would we ever get a wire rope to choke it off without it slipping?

Then as I walked around the coral head, I noticed it had two stalks holding it up with a narrow passage in between them. I explained to topside the situation, then told green diver to fetch the wire strap. This coral head was larger than most, about the size of a small dump truck. Green returned with the wire, handed it over to me, and I told him to go to the opposite side. I would push it through to him, but I cautioned him, not to shackle into the wire to choke the stalk, until I am out from underneath. The passage through the coral was much longer than it appeared, and I had to squeeze well under, the coral before finally passing the wire to green diver.

That day the ocean was glass calm, but every eight to ten seconds a small two-to-three-foot ocean swell came through, that would lift the ship. We were using it to our advantage to break off the coral appendages. Before I could wiggle out of the narrow passage, I felt the wire lift off the bottom. Green diver was so excited, he shackled in to choke before I could get out.

The wire now came tight across my chest which pinned me up against the coral as the ship rose. It became tighter and tighter, nearly squeezing the life out of me. In a fraction of a second, the pain was excruciating. Although I had nothing left in my lungs to scream, my mind said, *"Please no, please no."* I knew that if the ship went up just a few more inches, I would be crushed to death, or even cut in half.

As the swell went by and the wire slackened, I wiggled out as quickly as possible before the next wave came. The job was complete, and we both returned to the surface. I didn't say anything to my diving partner, or to master diver Paul. But later that day, I sat in silence and reflected about the entire incident. I realized that I was past my prime, and I needed to step aside for a younger generation of divers. Life was both precious and fragile, but it could be taken away with a single breath.

CHAPTER 22

BAD DAY

Three decades of being a Navy diver had taken its toll on my body. I'd had multiple orthopedic surgeries, and now I was scheduled for a shoulder replacement. I wanted some answers about my physical condition, and the orthopedic surgeon promised that after my surgery, he was going to bring in a pathologist to inspect the bone that he was removing.

I woke up in post-op and looked up at my surgeon and a pathologist, who was holding his laptop. On it were diagonal views of the bone that was removed and he asked me how many times I'd been treated for decompression sickness.

I answered, "None, but I was treated several times for omitted decompression." That's a condition that occurs when a diver skips a decompression stop while returning to the surface. The photos looked like someone sprinkled rock salt on the bone cutaways, and the pathologist told me I had bone necrosis. I asked if it was just in my shoulder, and he said, unfortunately it would be throughout my body.

My surgeon saw my eyes welling up and he said, "Rick, we will deal with the issues as they come up. It just means you may need more joint replacements in the future." He then suggested that I should avoid any impact or contact sports, which included running, and the pathologist added, no diving.

"But I can spearfish, can't I?" I asked, and the pathologist replied, "Absolutely not."

Then, in a much louder voice, I responded, "You might as well just give me a shot right now, if you take spearfishing away from me."

My surgeon knew me well and explained to the pathologist that I was a free diver, and only held my breath to spearfish. They both agreed that I could continue the sport.

My surgeon suggested that I remain in a warm climate and the warmer the better. Angela had been after me for years to move to Australia so we moved to Tropical Northern Queensland Australia.

Months of shoulder rehab passed, and I could feel my body stiffening up, so I went to my local gym to see what Yoga or Pilates classes looked like. I poked my head into a yoga class and there were a dozen scantily clad women holding their bodies in positions that didn't look natural. I thought, *way too flexible for me.* Then I watched a Pilates class, and it was all women as well, but it looked more my speed.

I waited to talk to the instructor, but she told me her class was full, and to check back the following month. As I was walking out of the gym, I saw an ad on the bulletin board for Muay Thai classes, and I thought I would like to give that a try. I took the number down, and later that evening gave Glenn, the instructor, a call and said I wanted to try Muay Thai. His first question was about my age. I told him I was fifty-five and his answer was that I was too old.

I told him I was in the military for thirty-two years and a disabled veteran, but quite fit for a fifty-five-year-old. However, he didn't want the liability of training someone my age. The next day he called me back and agreed to train me privately. He said he couldn't sleep all night because he felt that he turned his back on a disabled veteran. I had a large garage at my house, and he said we could do the lessons there.

The first day Glenn came over to train me, he noticed my boat and the row of spearguns, and asked what spearfishing was all about? I told him that the best spearfishing in the world was just twenty-five miles away, and he mentioned he always wanted to learn. From that point on, Glenn was teaching me Muay Thai, and I was teaching him how to spearfish.

One day after a Muay Thai lesson he asked me when I was diving next. I replied, "Tomorrow, but in-shore for barramundi and fingermark." He asked if he could go and I said, "I need to check with Pete, the boat owner, but I don't see why not." I also told him that visibility wouldn't be very good, not like it was miles offshore.

On our way to meet Pete, early the next morning, he asked me how I dealt with diving in dirty water, knowing there were probably sharks there.

"Well, I haven't been hit by lightning yet. In fact, you could get hit by twenty-two lightning bolts before getting bitten by a single shark."

"I guess that makes me feel better," Glenn said, then added: "I hope I don't get hit by lightning today." We both laughed and continued our drive down to the Cardwell boat ramp about forty miles south of my home.

Glenn had been diving for just eight months and it wasn't surprising that he would be concerned about sharks. I'd swum numerous times in waters with multiple sharks, some of them quite aggressive, but I'd never been bitten.

When we arrived, Pete and his friend, Aaron, had the boat in the water and were waiting for us. I introduced Glenn and we were off. We tried three or four of our best spots, but the water was so dirty we couldn't dive them.

I mentioned that I thought a rocky island, called Eva Rock, might be clearer, and that there was a massive cave that went under the rock and came out the other side. Inside the cave we might find some fingermark or barramundi.

When we arrived at the island and anchored, the water underneath the boat looked clearer than what we had experienced so far. We all slipped into the water, and I took Glenn over to the rock. We both dove down, and I showed him the cave. The water was only fifteen feet deep on each side of the cave, and very clear. You can see right through to the other side, as it was big enough to drive a truck through it. It also looked like some nice fish were inside.

Glenn and I returned to the surface, and I said, "How cool was that?" I told him that Pete and I were going to dive down to a nearby ledge that was about forty-five feet deep, and Aaron would go down to the cave with him. Aaron speared a fish very quickly, and took it to the boat, which was about twenty feet from the rock. Then he swam out to where Pete and I were diving, about forty feet from the rock.

We'd only been diving for a few minutes, when Pete came up and said he saw a large bull shark. I dove immediately and raced down only to see the back half of the shark, but it was an adult female approximately twelve to thirteen feet long.

I returned to the surface and said to Pete and Aaron. "Let's not risk it. Besides, not many fish around. Let's get going."

The boat wasn't far away, but I couldn't see Glenn where I'd left him. While the two guys swam back to the boat, I decided to look on the opposite side of the rock for Glenn. I spotted him on that side of the cave entrance and thought he was probably having fun with the fish inside.

I turned to go back to the boat, but then heard an unusual noise. I stopped and went back to glance at Glenn, and saw his body being shaken from side to side like a rag doll. I screamed for Pete and Aaron to get into the boat. I bolted for the boat as fast as I could swim and I don't know how, but I was in the boat before them. I bellowed at them to cut the anchor line and I grabbed the controls to desperately get to the opposite side of the rock.

I raced around the rock to find a massive area of crimson stained water, about the size of our boat, but no Glenn. Then suddenly we saw the back of his head bob up, but he remained facedown. I maneuvered the boat alongside him and told Pete and Aaron to grab him. As they lifted him into the boat, I could see his entire thigh was hanging off him, and all that was left was his femur. I cried out as loud as I could: "FUCK, FUCK, FUCK," and directed them to lay him down. He was a pale ash color and lifeless.

I knew what to do from years of improved explosive device (IED) medical training. I removed my weight belt and stripped everything off. Then I fastened it on his upper thigh as tight as I could. He was still lifeless, grey, and unresponsive. I shouted for Pete to get us home, and for Aaron to call the emergency number 000. Then I saw the faintest amount of blood coming out of his femoral artery. I removed Glenn's weight belt, stripped it, and fastened it even higher above the previous one.

I knew when I was placing the second tourniquet on, it would seal the fate of Glenn's leg. But at this point, I was just trying to save his life. I was able to get the second weight belt around his leg twice, before locking it down as tightly as I could. The moment it was sinched, blood stopped flowing out of his femoral artery, and Glenn's color changed. Then he screamed.

In the military, we are instructed that in a life and death situation, pain is a good thing, and to keep the patient awake no matter what. On the ride in, I was doing everything in my power to keep Glenn awake, which included rubbing his sternum aggressively, and even slapping him just as hard as I could. I kept telling him over and over he was not going to die, and that he had to live for Jesse Lee and his three kids.

Besides Glenn's thigh being shredded from his femur, he also had a massive eight-inch gash on his calf. It looked as if the shark had swallowed Glenn's fin, and leg down its throat, before biting down on his upper thigh. The bite went completely around the circumference of his upper thigh. I put Glenn's thigh muscle and flesh back over his femur, and covered it with my shirt, so he wouldn't see the injury. Then I treated him for shock, cradling him in my arms, and not letting him close his eyes. I kept him awake for the entire trip back to the boat ramp. I also lifted his unaffected leg, elevating it so the blood would pool in his core.

EMS crews met us on the pier but were not prepared for what they saw. They immediately radioed in for an Emergency Life Flight helicopter. An argument ensued between the EMS team leader and the helicopter pilot, who wanted to land at a town thirty miles away. The EMS chief said, "If you don't come here, he won't make it."

I stayed with Glenn during the ambulance ride, and once the Life Flight Helicopter landed, I was invited to make the journey with them to Cairns Hospital. After four to five hours in surgery, the doctor came out to brief the family. She exclaimed Glenn was not out of the woods yet, and it would be touch and go for several days.

She then said Glenn would lose a portion of his leg, hopefully only his foot. Everybody gasped and the doctor said, "Why wouldn't you think he would lose a portion of his leg? When did the tourniquet go on?"

I replied 0930. Then she said, "There is also a great deal of damage under the tourniquets," and everyone in the room looked at me. I felt like crawling into a hole and was worried I had done something wrong. The doctor saw everyone looking at me and said, "No, no, no. If he hadn't done his job so well, we wouldn't be having this conversation right now."

After the doctor spoke to Glenn's wife, Jesse Lee, and his parents, she came over to me and asked where I learned how to apply a tourniquet. I told her I was in the US Navy, and we trained relentlessly on IED casualties, specifically lower leg trauma and I knew I only had three minutes to save his life. She smiled, gave me a hug and said, "Amazing job. He only lost four units of blood."

Later that evening, the doctors introduced blood back into Glenn's repaired leg, but his body rejected it. To save his life, they amputated his right leg about six inches down from his groin.

Three days after Glenn's shark attack, I went back out to Eva Rock, a very isolated rocky outcrop in the center of miles and miles of white sand, and nothingness. Bull sharks can be very territorial. They stay put if they have an abundant easy food source. I talked to a couple of commercial fishermen who said there was a large bull shark at Eva that had been terrorizing fishermen by stealing everything they caught. I asked them how to find it. They told me to go to the northside of the island, anchor in fifty feet of water, and rev up the engine.

The visibility at the rocks was crystal clear, and I followed their instructions. After anchoring, I loaded my speargun, revved the 250-horsepower outboard, and minutes later I was staring at her just twenty feet below my boat. The big girl made eye contact with me and slowly started swimming straight up, only to find my loaded four-banded tuna gun pointing right at her.

For the first time in her life, she was now being hunted, and when the 3/8-inch shaft impacted her in the head, she never knew what hit her. At least her ending was over quickly. A few people were upset at me for doing it and made comments like: "The shark had every right to bite Glenn. After all, he was in their environment." My answer to that was: "True, and I have every right to kill it for attacking my friend."

Glenn was in a coma for a week, and once he was stable enough, they woke him up. His family was there and of course everyone was telling him he would be okay, and how much they loved him. I stayed out in the hall and waited for all the crying to be over, but then overheard Glenn ask where I was.

I walked in and gave him a hug and said, "You have plenty of people telling you everything is going to be okay. I won't, but what I will tell you is to get the hell out of that bed when you're ready. Now do you want to see the shark that bit you?"

My phone had more than twenty pictures of my excursion back to EVA Rock. At first, Glenn thought I had pictures of the day he was attacked, but I said: "No, these are just from two days ago while you were in coma. I went back and found that shark."

From that point on, my relationship with Glenn changed to more like an uncle and nephew. I have been with him every step of the way, and now he is a successful businessman and has four beautiful children.

Glenn tells the story of what happened that day from his point of view in the appendix.

CHAPTER 23

I SURVIVED

I could no longer open my eyes, nor could I feel my arms or my legs. My heart was barely beating, but I could feel the boat pounding through the waves. I could hear the roar of the motor as the driver tried to will the boat to go faster. Finally, the boat slowed, and the pounding faded away. I felt a jolt as the boat was slammed into reverse, and people shouted back and forth. I was ashore after an agonizing ninety minutes.

I knew I was in a bad way. Nearly all my blood were puddled in the back of the boat, and my leg was shredded from the shark attack. I slipped into blackness. I was pulseless and unresponsive upon arrival.

The emergency crews were organized and waiting for me. They knew it was going to be bad, that it was a life-or-death situation. Firefighters got me out of the boat and rushed me up to a tent, where EMS crews went to work to stop the bleeding and doctors prepared to squeeze precious blood back into my system. Whatever was in my tank was now gone.

The emergency crews on shore were nothing short of remarkable. They pulled me back from the edge of death. One doctor was standing by to paddle me to restart my heart, while the other was working feverishly to get an IV into a collapsed artery.

Once the blood hit my heart, it started my whole system. Like a possessed zombie, I sat up and said, "Get off my leg you are hurting me." My sudden movement and voice startled everyone around me. A female emergency medical technician had her fist buried into the left side of my groin, to stop the bleeding. A firefighter was lifting her off the ground by her ankles so she could put the maximum amount of force through her fist to slow what blood was left.

My wife and my best friend, Mark, showed up just as they were carrying me into the life flight turbo helicopter. They had to drive through dozens of spectators and news crews, to get to the awaiting chopper. Before Mark could even stop the Landcruiser, Angela bolted out of the door. When police officers grabbed her, she screamed: "He is my husband, let me go!"

Finally, the doctors said she could see me, but she needed to hurry. She hugged me and whispered in my ear, "You need to make it through this Rick. Don't you quit on me and the boys. You fight."

Once in the air, it was a race to see if they could get me to the hospital before I ran out of fluids again. The doctor at the boat ramp not only had the foresight to bring as much blood as was available, but she also brought several bags of saline solution in case there wasn't enough. She told the Life Flight doctor that if he ran out of blood to start pumping the saline solution into me.

Halfway to the hospital, I went into cardiac arrest and was paddled by the Life Flight doctor, then injected with just saline to keep me alive. "You gotta go faster, gotta go faster," the doctor shouted at the pilot. They had to get me to the hospital before I ran out of blood a second time.

I was delivered as a Code Red Blanket patient. That's a rapid transfer protocol, that fast tracks trauma patients with severe blood loss, directly into the operating theatre, it's only utilized for the most severe life and death cases.

Meanwhile, I was elsewhere.

Darkness, darkness everywhere, but where was I? It was peaceful, warm, and unthreatening, much like being in a womb before birth. I felt a sense of euphoria. I was comfortable and it was very serene, but where was I? Was I dead? No, I could feel my heartbeat. Was I under water? No, I could feel gravity. But where was I?

It was as if I was searching for a well-known house in total darkness, feeling my way along the walls to search each room for answers. But no answers came, just darkness and serenity. It seems I should have felt some anxiety, even panic. After all, I was in the dark and didn't know where I was. Yet, I remained calm and at peace.

Then I felt energy around me. It was like a wave of electric current tingling my body. It didn't feel like it came from one source but from several. It was intense, powerful, yet loving and caring. Then I saw them: glowing orbs of light, like fireflies, were all around me. They didn't frighten me, rather they were very comforting. I was in a tranquil state and experiencing inexplicable bliss in the presence of these orbs, which I knew were beings.

I've heard about these near-death experiences where people see a tunnel and a bright light at the end of it, or the light coming toward them, but my experience was different. The spirits, souls, guides—whatever they were—appeared only about as bright as night lights. I felt a strong desire to move closer, and they became a bit brighter. I felt like I was in a counsel of ethereal beings, a jury of light and love.

I wanted to stay in their presence, but a voice said, "Go home." Then another male voice spoke more forcefully, "Go home, Rick." I was confused, uncertain. This place, wherever it was, felt safe, like a harbor in a storm. But I was told to go back.

At that moment, I heard an alarm go off. A strange woman's voice bellowed, "This bloody heart rate monitor is set at forty beats per minute, and he keeps holding his breath."

I felt someone gently touch my arm, and I heard a voice I recognized as my wife, Angela. She told the nurse that I was used to holding my breath, that I'd been a diver my whole life.

Then Angela leaned in close to me, I could feel the warmth of her face as she said, "Rick, just *breathe*," and I woke up!

I found out that I'd been put into an induced coma, as they began the emergency surgery to save my life. The lead doctor initially was going to keep me in a coma but decided to wake me up after the surgery to find out if I was brain dead.

They were concerned about that possibility, because when I reached shore after the attack, I had no blood left in my body, resulting in a multitude of heart attacks. Also, the blood I was given was generic "super blood," which can become toxic with just four to six units. They gave me fourteen units. When I was awakened from the coma, I knew everything about the attack. I also knew the birthdays of my two sons. With the knowledge that my brain was functioning, they put me back into the coma.

I remained in the coma the next day, when I underwent a massive surgery involving thirty doctors, as they put my leg back together. After that surgery, I was awakened. That was when I returned from my voyage to the Other Side and found Angela waiting for me. I was in the ICU for five days and had four surgeries. The other two surgeries that week were skin grafts.

I was supposed to be in the hospital for two to six months, but I was ready to go home after just three weeks. One day, the doctor extended her hand and told me to stand. Within two days, I was able to walk without any assistance.

In February 2021, just four months after the attack, I went diving, and caught two large lobsters. Although I couldn't use a fin on my damaged leg, it was nice to get back in the water. I could still hold my breath, too, and stay under at least a couple of minutes.

In May, I had a fifth surgery. The day they saved my life, the doctors had clamped the perineal nerve which deadened my foot. The surgery moved some muscles and tendons so I can now pick up my foot instead of dragging it.

My condition now in August is very optimistic. I still walk with a limp, but it will get better with time. I am very fortunate to still have my leg, and more importantly, my life. I am so very grateful to be alive and especially grateful to everyone who helped save my life.

I sought out each and every first responder, fire fighter, emergency medical team member, life flight team, and all the doctors and nurses to thank them personally for doing the impossible and not giving up on me. My last comment to them was "you did not just save my life, you prevented my sons from growing up without a father, and for that I can never repay you enough."

APPENDIX 1

WHAT I REMEMBER

BY ANGELA BETTUA

That morning Rick left very early to go diving with his friend Pete, since the boat ramp they were departing from was at least an hour and a half away. It was still dark when he came back into the bedroom to kiss me goodbye and said that he would see me later. I barely moved because I was so tired, but I never worried about him diving as he has been a waterman all his life. He owned a boat before he owned a car. He left and I fell back asleep with the kids.

It was a normal, usual Sunday. Yet, I felt uneasy. Something was nagging me, though, and I couldn't figure it out. Then my phone rang and I saw Pete's number on my caller ID. Rick usually calls me from a friend's phone because he sometimes leaves his phone in his truck or the battery is flat. I answered the phone expecting to hear Rick's voice, but it was Pete's.

"Ange, I've transferred Rick onto a bigger boat, he's been bitten by a shark!"

"Oh, fuck off, Pete!"

"I'm serious, Ang."

"Are you fucking kidding me, Pete?"

"No, I'm not Ang."

I could hear the urgency in his voice. I was in the living room, and I looked over to my two young boys, oblivious to the emergency unfolding as they played on their iPads. I hurried into my bedroom, closed the door, and I asked him, "Pete, this is very important. Do you think he is going to make it?"

"No."

I just remember panic bubbling up from my gut to my throat. I didn't yell or cry, I just said, "Fuck!" I felt stunned. He told me to head to Dungeness boat ramp in Lucinda, that they would be there in ninety minutes. It would take me longer than that. After getting directions, I decided to call Rick's best friend Mark, and surprisingly he answered his phone on the first ring. I told him what had happened and that I needed help getting to Rick.

He was out the door before we even hung up, on his way to get me. Then I had to find a friend to mind the kids, while I went to see their dad. Our friend came, and I said as calmly as I could to the boys, that I needed to go help dad with something important, and I would be right back. They said okay, and I left.

Mark drove fast, yet carefully; all the while I was praying and making deals with God. Just let him be okay, and I won't ever complain about him being a pain in my ass again.

When we got to the ramp, dozens of people with their camera phones trying to get footage of Rick, but the police and EMS had sheets up, hiding him from view. Mark drove as close as he could toward the sheet. I jumped out before he came to a full stop, but police blocked me. I told them that Rick was my husband, but they still held me back. I could see him on the gurney, and he looked peaceful. I asked one of the EMTs if I could please hug him and give him a kiss.

I was told to hurry up, this was a very critical situation and every second mattered. I walked up to him, looked at his body and saw his leg. It was wrapped up in some clear material, like cling wrap. I saw a sliced area, and I could see muscle and fat. I looked up at his face and leaned in and hugged him. "I whispered in his ear that he needed to make it. "Don't you quit; fight."

"Is he going to make it?" I asked a doctor. His look said no, that I was probably seeing him alive for the last time. The EMT shouted that they needed to leave NOW!

I backed away and saw them lifting him into the helicopter. Mark grabbed me and said we needed to go. We had another hour drive to get to the hospital in Townsville. We drove away before the helicopter lifted off.

We arrived at the hospital, and I saw the helicopter, surrounded by news reporters and cameras. Mark saw the horror on my face, and he told me not to worry. He brought me in a back way to avoid the media circus. After checking in, we went into a private waiting room where I was told how dire the situation was, that the likelihood of Rick not making it was very high.

Everything was explained to me by trauma surgeons, neurosurgeons, a plastic surgeon, and orthopedic surgeons. I was told that he had a massive cardiac arrest in the chopper as well. I was told the amount of blood they transfused was so much that his vital organs would be damaged, or that he would be brain dead. My thoughts kept crossing over to my children, especially my youngest, Derek, who is Rick's shadow. His father is his hero. How would I tell them they will never see their dad again? Rick and I are like oil and vinegar. He is very military, very structured, and methodical. I am more easy-going and a jokester. How would I be able to assume this dual role now?

Sitting in the waiting room felt like purgatory. Every time a surgeon would enter, the look of dread on their faces told me his chances of survival were minimal. Finally, I was told there was nothing more they could do. My heart sank and I looked at our friend, Cameron, who is a retired military man with the Australian Army. He had rushed over as soon as he heard what happened. His eyes were wide and they were welling up with tears as he looked at me. I remember him hugging me tightly and we were sure that the next words were that he hadn't made it through surgery.

I was told that the trauma was so severe, that putting him through any more surgery at this point would more than likely hinder his chances, and that he was placed into an induced coma. I was told he would be in a coma for at least four days. They reiterated that Rick was very sick, that he was in the intensive care unit.

I asked them what should I do now? Could I see him? The two surgeons looked at each other and told me to wait a little while, they would call me when I was able to see Rick. They also said they knew we had two young children, that I should go home and come back tomorrow with them. I was certain it was for us to say goodbye.

Mark, Cameron, and I were sent to a waiting room outside the ICU ward. It was quiet, and empty. Due to Covid, only two people were allowed into ICU within a twenty-four-hour period. Cameron said he was okay to wait until tomorrow to see him, that Mark should go with me.

We were buzzed in and walked through what seemed like a maze of hallways. We approached a figure on the bed, covered up, except for the head which looked plastic, and lifeless. I thought for a second that it was Rick but as we got closer, we realized it was a practice dummy. My relief was overwhelming and it was the first time Mark and I laughed.

We turned a corner and were told where we would find Rick. The curtains surrounding his bed were opened for us. Rick was in a coma with multiple tubes coming out of his body. I walked up to him, stroked his hair, and touched his face. I don't know if he knew I was there, but again I whispered in his ear. "You're going to fight, Rick. I don't know how we will live without you. Please make it through this. For us. For you."

Mark was by the foot of the bed. He asked if we could see his leg. The ICU nurse looked at me, and I said I wanted to see it too. Mark pulled the sheet over and all we could see was that he was heavily bandaged from his mid-calf to his hip. Mark grabbed his foot.

"Ange, I think his leg is going to be saved. His foot feels warm, I can feel a pulse." Mark was so optimistic. He never gave up on Rick coming out of this alive and fully intact. Maybe he did it so I could feel positive, maybe for himself. Mark has suffered a lot of loss in his life and I'm sure he didn't want me to feel that same pain.

I said goodbye and had another long look at Rick. I left dreading the three-hour drive home thinking about what to tell the boys and getting our affairs in order. I decided I'd tell them in the morning. I called my friend Nina to check on them, and to let her know we were coming home.

As we were driving, I received a call from one of the surgeons. He told me that they wanted to raise him out of the coma so they could check his cognitive abilities. They would call back when they had the results. I said okay and prayed. About forty-five minutes later, I received the follow-up call. The surgeon was very excited, and said that they had woken Rick up, and although he couldn't talk, because of all the tubes coming out of his mouth, he was able to answer with motions to their questions. He knew who he was, he knew where he was, he knew what had happened to him, and he knew he had a wife and two children.

He told me that he was extremely happy with Rick's cognitive abilities, and that they put him back in to a coma. I got home late that night and tried my best to sleep. I told my kids that dad was still fishing, we would see him tomorrow. They weren't phased by that, since they are used to Rick going away on long range fishing trips.

The next morning, I gathered things to take with me to Townsville, uncertain if I was going to stay there overnight. That's when I got a phone call from the surgeon. He said they decided to wake Rick up from the coma so they could work on saving his leg. I was surprised and was standing in exactly the same spot in my bedroom as when Pete told me Rick was not going to make it. Now I was getting the opposite message, and of course I was elated. They told me they wouldn't wake him for a few hours. Good, enough time for me to be there with the boys. Not an hour later I got a call from the nurse. "Hello Angela, would you like to speak to Rick?"

"What? Yes! Oh my God, he's awake?"

"Yes. He can't speak but I can tell you what he gestures."

She put the phone to his ear, I said, "Rick! I love you so much! The boys and I are coming right now! You make sure you hang in there for us, you need to cowboy the fuck up!" He always used that term on me, finally I got my chance to say it to him. The nurse got back on the phone, and said he gave me a thumbs up.

After a few hurdles, we finally made it to the hospital. I had prepared the kids for what they were going to see. I had told them before we left, that daddy had been attacked by a shark, but he was going to be okay. They asked if he was going to be like "Uncle" Glenn, our friend who lost his leg to a shark. I told them I didn't know. They really didn't care. Dad was alive, that was all that mattered. We arrived at hospital and Rick was heavily sedated, but he was awake.

I went in to see him alone first, just to make sure everything was okay. He looked at me as I walked toward him and he said, "It happened so fast, I couldn't stop it." When he started to reach down to feel for his leg, I told him he still had his leg. A smile washed over his face and he closed his eyes.

I held his hand and I knew after that he would be okay. I was told he would probably be at hospital for six months for his recovery. But he was home within three weeks. Rick made sure of that. He's an anomaly, a superman as his former rear admiral called him. He was almost sixty years old and survived a "Code Red Blanket," defying the odds. But that was just classic Rick.

APPENDIX 2

ANOTHER SURVIVOR

BY GLENN DICKSON

I woke up early feeling excited, knowing I was going free diving and spearfishing with "Uncle Rick", and getting out on the water. I was feeling a little anxious at the same time, though, because it was a new dive spot. I got into my truck and picked up Rick for the forty-five-minute drive to Cardwell.

En route, as we talked about our plans for the day. I had a moment of anxiety about the dangers we faced every time we dive, namely sharks! I asked Rick if he had any fears of getting attacked, and he replied, "You can get hit by lightning twenty times before getting bitten by one shark, and we haven't been hit by lightning even once yet."

That made me feel more at ease again, and we went back to talking about the chances of bringing home a prize fish to fulfill our hunting instincts and to please our families with our success.

We arrived at the Port Hinchinbrook boat ramp where I was introduced to Peter and Aaron, who were Rick's friends and diving buddies. We were all excited to be away from work and going out on a magical day to the in-shore reefs around Hinchinbrook Island. We travelled approximately forty-five minutes before arriving at the first dive location, which was a very shallow shipwreck. It was immediately obvious that the water was very dirty. I could hardly see the tip of my speargun once I entered the water. We decided to leave the location and look for a spot with clearer water.

We finally anchored east of the main Hinchinbrook Island at a spot, known as "Eva Rock," which was supposed to be an excellent location for the fish we desired. Unbeknownst to me, it was also known for being a very "sharky" location. We didn't waste any time, and all jumped into the cold salty water. We loaded our guns and began the hunt. The water was much clearer here. I could see ten to fifteen feet around me, and all the way to the bottom. The improved visibility made me feel more at ease. I could see whatever was around me.

The group split into pairs, and we proceeded to dive near the pinnacle of rock which has a big cave underneath. It was teaming with life. My dive partner, Aaron, managed to shoot a mangrove jack, and wanted to get it into the boat to secure the catch, and avoid carrying around potential shark bait.

I stayed in the dive location, which was only twenty feet from the anchored boat, and continued diving. I went to the bottom and comfortably slowed my heart, relaxed, and enjoyed the beauty of the ocean. I saw a shadowy figure under a rock that I thought might be a mangrove jack. I took aim and shot. The spear struck slightly behind the fish's brain, which caused it to shudder about in a manic state. I knew that was a dinner bell for predators. As I began to rise to the surface, the fish continued swimming erratically. I came to the surface on the opposite side of the rock, instead of near the boat where I'd entered the cave.

I grabbed the spear and pulled the fish toward me. I took out my dive knife and spiked it directly into its brain. BANG! At that moment, I was struck violently, shaken like a rag doll, then pulled under water. It was a fast and extremely powerful force shaking me, tearing deep into the flesh of my right leg. I knew it was a shark and I knew I was in extreme danger.

The shock was immense. I couldn't feel any pain, I just knew I was damaged badly and could die. The shaking suddenly stopped and everything went into slow motion. I immediately knew that if I had any chance, it was to swim with everything I had left, and get to the rock, which was steep, and covered in barnacles, but only ten feet away. I was on the opposite side of the rock from the boat.

I started swimming, which felt like I was carrying a dead

weight. It was my torn and damaged limb flopping around behind me, as I used my remaining limbs to reach for the rock. It took an eternity and as I reached for the rock, BANG!

I was struck again, pulled under, and shaken before being let go. The shark had taken another piece of the same limb. I was in serious trouble, and tried to yell to Rick, but my voice was like a screeching gurgle. It was enough to get Rick's attention.

Then I had the feeling of being carried, which put me into a sense of ease, knowing I was no longer in the water with the massive predator. I'm a martial arts instructor, but now I was about to have the biggest fight of my entire life.

I was lying on the floor of the boat unconscious, and bleeding out. Rick demanded that Aaron lift my leg so he could put a torniquet on it, which ultimately saved my life. Rick not only placed one tourniquet on me, but also a second one, to completely stop the bleeding. Peter and Aaron seemed to be in shock and unsure of what to do. Rick, on the other hand, went into full military mode and took control of the situation. He ordered Aaron and Peter to contact emergency services, and get the boat back to shore, while he did everything he could to save my life.

I couldn't feel pain in my leg as the nerves were completely lacerated. But the pain was transferred to my back, where I'd been previously injured. It was so agonizing that I could hardly breathe. I screamed for Rick to hold my back up to ease my pain. Every breath was shallow and getting shallower.

Rick cradled me in his arms the whole way back, screaming at me to stay awake, and telling me over and over that I would make it. But I began to feel cold, very cold. I lost a lot of blood, and the world around me was getting smaller and smaller. Each time I would close my eyes Rick would scream at me to open them, even slapping me to stay awake.

Dying was the easiest option compared to facing the reality of my situation; my daughter's face came to mind. She was looking at me with her beautiful smile, as if to say, "Dad, it's not time yet, we need you."

It was at this moment that my fight response kicked into high gear. Years of pain and hardship and emotional challenges being a Muay-Thai fighter were triggered. Suddenly, my soul re-entered my body and I was awakened with a goal of survival, a goal of fighting my way back home, at least to give my beautiful fiancé Jessie-Lee one last kiss.

Being a fitness professional, I knew that controlling my heart rate would help me take control of my thoughts. Rick was talking to me, comforting me, and letting me know that I would not only survive, but make it home to see my family. The ride to the boat ramp felt like the longest trip of my life. Forty-five minutes felt like an eternity, but I was determined to make it.

The remainder of the trip came to me in pulsing visions of black and white surroundings, awareness of Rick close by, and the voices telling me to stay awake and fight on. I woke as we neared the harbor, and I felt sharp pains, as the bounce of the boat rippled through my lower back. Sounds were muffled, but I heard: "We are nearing help, Glenn!"

I perked up a little knowing land was near. As soon as we arrived, a paramedic team went to work stabilizing me over the next hour while we waited for the helicopter that was bringing blood. I felt a drill pierce into my right shoulder, and I kept trying to respond to the paramedic, while he filled me with fluid to keep my remaining blood circulating.

The helicopter arrived, and I started to believe I had a chance of making it. They weren't going to let anyone else on the helicopter, but I demanded that Rick be allowed to join us. When the pilot realized Rick's military and emergency medical background, he was told he could come along. The trip on the helicopter was an out-of-body experience. The drugs subdued the pain, but they also sent me on a trip into space, and back into the ocean! Rick held my hand the whole way. I woke here and there demanding more drugs to take me away from the reality of my situation. All the while Rick kept his eyes locked on mine, telling me I was going to live. I knew I could make it now, not just to say goodbye, but to survive and be able to see my children grow up.

As we landed and the paramedics started rolling me toward the hospital, I yelled: "I will survive!" with every bit of energy I could muster. My parents were there waiting for me, and they approached in horror and disbelief, with deep sadness. I told them it was okay, that I would make it. Suddenly, Jessie-Lee came running into the emergency room and I asked for a kiss.

I hoped it wasn't the last kiss, and fortunately it wasn't. I lost my leg, but the doctors saved my life. Without Rick's help, though, I would not have made it to the hospital.

ABOUT THE AUTHOR

Master Chief Rick Bettua served thirty years as a U.S. Navy diver, enlisting at age seventeen in 1979. He finished his career in 2008 as a Command Master Chief Petty Officer and Master Diver, then returned for another three-year stint as an advisor, retiring in 2011. He qualified as a Master Diver in 1991 and was promoted early to Master Chief Petty Officer in 1995.

In October 2004, he became the Command Master Chief of Mobile Diving Salvage Unit One (MDSU-1) in Hawaii. In that role, he managed the world's largest and most diverse diving command with more than 250 personnel operating throughout the Pacific and Indian Oceans as well as Iraq and Kuwait.

As a Surface Warfare Specialist, he served in Desert Storm, Desert Freedom, Operation Iraqi Freedom and Operation Enduring Freedom. His awards include: Meritorious Service Medal (2 awards), Navy Commendation Medal (5 awards), Air Force Life Saving Medal and the Navy Achievement Medal (8 awards).

Master Chief Bettua has three sons, Nicholas, Troy and Derek and has been married to Angela since March 2006.

Rob MacGregor is a *New York Times* bestselling author of twenty-one novels and nineteen non-fiction books in the New Age and self-help field. His novel *Prophecy Rock* won the Edgar Allan Poe Award for mystery writing. He has worked with George Lucas, Peter Benchley and Billy Dee Williams. He has researched anomalous phenomena for many of his books, including seven Indiana Jones sagas and two remote viewing novels. He resides in Florida. He also teaches yoga classes and leads meditation workshops.

Curious about other Crossroad Press books?
Stop by our site:
http://store.crossroadpress.com
We offer quality writing
in digital, audio, and print formats.

CPSIA information can be obtained
at www.ICGtesting.com
Printed in the USA
LVHW100721020722
722553LV00024B/88/J